Integrated Korean

Intermediate 1

KLEAR Textbooks in Korean Language

Integrated Korean

Intermediate 1

Third Edition

Young-mee Cho   Hyo Sang Lee   Carol Schulz   Ho-min Sohn   Sung-Ock Sohn

University of Hawai'i Press
Honolulu

© 2020 University of Hawai'i Press
All rights reserved
Printed in China
25 24 23 22 21   6 5 4 3 2

This textbook series has been developed by the Korean Language Education and Research Center (KLEAR) with the support of the Korea Foundation.

Library of Congress Cataloging-in-Publication Data
Names: Cho, Young-mee Yu, author. | Lee, Hyo Sang, author. | Schulz, Carol
  (Carol H.), author. | Sohn, Ho-min, author. | Sohn, Sung-Ock S., author.
Title: Integrated Korean. Intermediate / Young-mee Cho, Hyo Sang Lee, Carol
  Schulz, Ho-min Sohn, Sung-Ock Sohn.
Other titles: KLEAR textbooks in Korean language.
Description: Third edition. | Honolulu : University of Hawai'i Press, 2020.
  | Series: KLEAR textbooks in Korean language
Identifiers: LCCN 2019058802 | ISBN 9780824886776 (v. 1 ; paperback) | ISBN
  9780824886820 (v. 2 ; paperback)
Subjects: LCSH: Korean language—Textbooks for foreign speakers—English.
Classification: LCC PL913 .C4843 2020 | DDC 495.782/421—dc23
LC record available at https://lccn.loc.gov/2019058802

Page design by Hyun Jun Lee
Illustrations by Seijin Han

Audio files for this volume may be downloaded in MP3 format at
https://kleartextbook.com.

Printer-ready copy has been provided by KLEAR.

University of Hawai'i Press books are printed on acid-free paper and meet the guidelines for permanence and durability of the Council on Library Resources

Contents

Preface to the Third Edition

The Integrated Korean (IK) inaugural volumes, *Beginning 1* and *Beginning 2*, of the Korean Language Education & Research Center (KLEAR) appeared in 2001. They were followed by *Intermediate, Advanced Intermediate* (now *High Intermediate*), *Advanced*, and *High Advanced* volumes. The IK series, especially the beginning and intermediate books, have attracted a large number of learners of Korean around the world, especially in the United States and other English-speaking countries. Currently, some one hundred universities and colleges use them for regular classroom instruction. The IK series is popular because the authors endeavored to develop each volume in accordance with performance-based principles and methodology: contextualization, learner-centeredness, use of authentic materials, usage-orientedness, balance between acquiring and using skills and, above all, the integration of speaking, listening, reading, writing, and culture. In addition, grammar points are systematically introduced with simple but adequate explanations and abundant examples and exercises.

Over the years, classroom teachers and students, as well as the authors themselves, noticed minor shortcomings in the first- and second-year volumes that called for improvement. Consequently, at the original authors' recommendation, a revision team was formed for the second edition consisting of Mee-Jeong Park (coordinator), Sang-Suk Oh, Joowon Suh, and Mary Shin Kim. With a strong commitment to offering the best possible learning opportunities, the team efficiently reorganized and restructured the material based on feedback received from an extensive survey. The second edition of the beginning and intermediate texts and their accompanying workbooks appeared in 2009–2013.

A few years ago a decision was made to improve and refine the intermediate volumes to anticipate the needs of today's students and instructors. The following revision team has taken on this task:

Mee-Jeong Park, University of Hawai'i at Mānoa (Coordinator)
Mary Shin Kim, University of Hawai'i at Mānoa
Joowon Suh, Columbia University
Seonkyung Jeon, University of California at Los Angeles

Several instructors of Korean at various universities in the United States, primarily University of Hawai'i alumni, have been brought on board to provide editorial support: Sooran Pak (University of Southern California), Hye Young Smith (UH Mānoa), Jason Sung (Kapi'olani Community College), and UH Mānoa doctoral students Meghan Delaney, Tyler Miyashiro, and HwanHee Kim.

The third edition of *Intermediate 1–2* differs from the second in the following respects: First, it features an attractive full-color design with new photos and illustrations; second, most of the conversations have been revised for more natural interactions within each theme-based context; third, some of the grammar points in lessons 1 through 4 have been rearranged to better reflect their level of difficulty; and fourth, the number of total lessons has been slightly reduced by removing lesson 13 and redistributing some of its grammar points to other lessons.

On behalf of KLEAR and the original authors of the intermediate volumes of Integrated Korean, I wholeheartedly thank the revision team for their tireless effort and dedication.

Ho-min Sohn
KLEAR President
March 2020

Objectives

Lesson 1 날씨와 계절 [Weather and Seasons]

Texts	Grammar
Conversation 1 어느 계절을 제일 좋아하세요?	1. Change of state: A.S.~어/아지다 'become, get to be' 2. Sentence ending ~잖아요. 'You know, . . .' (assuming agreement)
Conversation 2 날씨가 추워졌네요.	3. Noun-modifying form ~던 (retrospective) 4. Expressing speaker's wish: ~(으)면 좋겠다 5. N 때 'at the time of N'; ~(으)ㄹ 때 'when'
Narration 일기예보	
Culture	**Usage**
음력과 양력: The use of the lunar and solar (Gregorian) calendars	1. Describing weather 2. Indicating possibility and capability 3. Listening to weather forecasts

Lesson 2 옷과 유행 [Clothing and Fashion]

Texts	Grammar
Conversation 1 백화점에서 옷을 사려고 해요.	1. V.S.~(으)려고 'intending to'; V.S.~(으)려고 하다 'intend to' 2. V.S.~기(가) 쉽다/어렵다 'it is easy/difficult to . . .'
Conversation 2 요즘 짧은 치마가 유행이에요.	3. N1말고 N2 'not N1 but N2' 4. Expressions of permission and prohibition: V.S. ~어도/아도 되다; V.S.~(으)면 안 되다 5. ~(으)ㄴ/는/(으)ㄹ 것 같다 'it seems/looks like'
Narration 백화점 쇼핑	
Culture	**Usage**
한국의 의(衣)생활: The Korean life pertaining to clothes	1. Requesting, granting, and denying permission 2. Making plans 3. Describing physical appearance 4. Shopping

Lesson 3 여행 [Travel]

Texts	Grammar
Conversation 1 한국에 가게 됐어요.	1. ~게 되다: change or turn of events 2. ~(으)면 되다 'have only to . . .', 'All one needs is . . .'
Conversation 2 한국에 갔다 왔어요.	3. Doubling of ~었-: ~었었-/~았었-/~ㅆ었- 4. ~어/아 본 적(이) 있다/없다 'There has been an/no occasion of . . .' 5. ~(으)니까: expressing a reason or logical sequence
Narration 소피아의 한국 여행	

Culture	Usage
경주: The ancient capital of the Silla Kingdom	1. Calling a travel agency and buying an airline ticket 2. Talking about vacation and summer jobs 3. Describing past events 4. Skimming newspaper ads for airline tickets and travel information

Lesson 4 한국 생활 I [Life in Korea I]

Texts	Grammar
Conversation 1 인사동에 가는 길이에요.	1. ~는 길이다/~는 길에 '(be) on one's way' 2. ~거든요. 'You see, (because)~'
Conversation 2 소포를 부치려고 하는데요.	3. N(이)요. 'It is [noun]' 4. ~(으)려면 'if . . . intends to do' 5. ~어야/아야지요. 'definitely/indeed/surely should/ought to/have to'
Narration 우진이의 편지	
Culture	**Usage**
인사동	1. Using postal services 2. Giving a warning and seeking advice 3. Writing personal letters

Lesson 5 한국 생활 II [Life in Korea II]

Texts	Grammar
Conversation 1 방값도 싸고 괜찮아.	1. The intimate speech style ~어/아 2. ~(으)ㄴ/는 편이다 'It is more the case of . . . than the other'. 3. ~(으)ㄴ/는지 알다/모르다 'know/don't know whether (what, who, where, when) . . .'
Conversation 2 이사 온 지 얼마나 됐어요?	4. A: ~(으)ㄴ 지 얼마나 됐어요? 'How long has it been since . . . ?' B: ~(으)ㄴ 지 TIME SPAN(이/가) 됐어요. 'It has been . . . since . . .' 5. ~다가: transference of an action/state to another
Narration 스티브의 하숙방	
Culture	**Usage**
하숙과 자취	1. Searching for housing 2. Describing buildings and interiors 3. Initiating a conversation and introducing oneself 4. Giving compliments and responding to compliments

Lesson 6　대중 교통 [Public Transportation]

Texts	Grammar
Conversation 1 등산 갈 준비 다 됐니?	1. The plain style ~(는/ㄴ)다 2. The use of the plain style in speaking 3. V.S.~기로 하다 'plan to/decide to'
Conversation 2 관악산 입구까지 가 주세요.	4. Indirect quotation: ~다고 하다, ~(으/느)냐고 하다, 　~(으)라고 하다, ~자고 하다 5. 아무리 ~어도/아도 'no matter how . . .'
Narration　스티브의 일기	
Culture	**Usage**
주민등록증	1. Asking for and giving directions 2. Using public transportation 3. Making telephone calls 4. Writing a journal

Lesson 7　가게에서 [At a Store]

Texts	Grammar
Conversation 1 사과 한 상자에 얼마예요?	1. ~어/아 보이다 'someone/something appears . . ./ 　looks . . .' 2. Passive verbs 3. ~어/아 있다 'In the state of being . . .'
Conversation 2 여기 뭐 사러 왔어?	4. ~어/아 가지고 'because, since'; 'by doing/being' 5. ~는 데(에) 'in/for ~ing . . .'
Narration　동네 시장	
Culture	**Usage**
택배	1. Talking about food and making a shopping list 2. Making recipes 3. Expressing hesitation

Main Characters

Minji
Korean-Canadian

Mark Smith
*Major in
Korean Culture
Australian*

Michael Jung
*Freshman in
Computer
Korean American*

Sophia Wang
*Went to Korea
during the vacation*

Amy
Steve's housemate

Steve Wilson
*Living in a
boardinghouse
in Korea*

Main Characters

Woojin
*Korean American
from New York*

Dongsoo
*Friend of Steve
and Woojin*

Soobin Kim
*Steve's classmate
Jenny's roommate*

Woojin
*Living in a studio
near campus*

Yumi Kim
*Freshman
in Biology
Korean*

Sophia Wang
*Sophomore
in Econ
Chinese*

1과 날씨와 계절

Lesson 1 Weather and Seasons

Conversation 1 어느 계절을 제일 좋아하세요?

▶ 민지와 마크가 도서관 앞에서 이야기하고 있습니다.

Conversation 1

민지: 날씨가 많이 시원해졌지요?G1.1

마크: 네, 정말 시원해졌어요. 올해 여름은
　　　장마가 유난히 길어서 지겨웠어요.

민지: 여름이 끝나고 벌써 가을이 됐네요.
　　　마크 씨는 어느 계절을 제일 좋아하세요?

마크: 저는 봄이 제일 좋아요. 날씨도 따뜻하고,
　　　꽃도 많이 피잖아요.G1.2 민지 씨는요?

민지: 저는 스키도 탈 수 있고 방학도 길어서
　　　겨울이 더 좋아요.

마크: 아, 그래요? 그럼, 민지 씨는 겨울이
　　　기다려지겠네요.

민지: 네, 그렇지만 단풍 구경을 할 수 있어서
　　　가을도 좋아해요.
　　　참, 마크 씨, 10월에 설악산에 단풍 구경하러
　　　가는데 같이 안 갈래요?

마크: 단풍 구경이요? 그렇지 않아도 가 보고
　　　싶었는데 잘 됐네요.

▶ COMPREHENSION QUESTIONS

1. 지금은 어느 계절입니까?
2. 마크는 왜 봄을 제일 좋아합니까?
3. 겨울 방학이 깁니까, 여름 방학이 깁니까?
4. 민지는 왜 가을과 겨울을 좋아합니까?
5. 민지는 10월에 무엇을 하고 싶어합니까?

NEW WORDS

NOUN

공기	air
구름	cloud
기온	temperature
낮	daytime
단풍	fall foliage
런던	London
설악산	Seorak Mount
스파게티	spaghetti
야외	the outside
에어컨	air-conditioner
외국어	foreign language
유럽	Europe
음식값	food cost
장마	rainy season
전화비	phone bill
콘서트	concert
하늘	sky

VERB

기다려지다	to be wished
(구름이) 끼다	to get cloudy
낮아지다	to get lower
내려가다	to go down
되다	②to function, work
시원해지다	to become cooler
피다	to bloom

ADJECTIVE

낮다	to be low
맑다	to be clear
지겹다	to be boring

ADVERB

계속	continuously
유난히	particularly

SUFFIX

~잖아요	you know
~어/아지다	to become

NEW EXPRESSIONS

1. 시원하다 has a range of meanings from 'to be cool in temperature, be refreshing, inspiring' to 'to be pleasing and satisfying'. That is why this adjective can be used not only to describe cold water (시원한 물) but also to express the feeling of satisfaction when drinking hot tea or taking a warm bath. Some examples are shown below:

시원한 바람	a cool, refreshing breeze
시원한 주스	a cool, refreshing juice
숙제를 다 해서 시원하다.	A load is off my mind after I finish my homework.
시원하게 말하다	to get right to the point

2. The month of October is often written with an Arabic number as in 10월. It is spelled and pronounced as 시월 and not 십월.

3. 잘 됐네요.　　　　　That's great, that's good news (it turned out well).
　 마침 잘 됐네요.　　 That's great (it turned out well) just in time.

Grammar

G1.1　　Change of state: A.S.~어/아지다 'become, get to be'

(1)　A:　벌써 겨울이네요.
　　　B:　감기 조심하세요. 이번 주부터 날씨가 추**워져요**.

(2)　A:　방이 참 깨끗**해졌네요**.
　　　B:　너무 더러워서 오랜만에 청소 좀 했어요.

(3)　A:　요즘 런던 날씨가 어때요?
　　　B:　계속 구름이 껴 있었는데 주말부터 맑**아질** 거예요.

(4)　A:　서울에 차가 참 많**아졌지요**?
　　　B:　네, 정말 운전하기 힘들**어졌어요**.

(5)　A:　오늘 서울 날씨가 어때요?
　　　B:　기온이 많이 낮**아졌어요**.

Examples

✤ Notes

1. This construction, attached to an adjective stem (A.S.), expresses a change from one state or condition to another. This construction changes an adjective into a verb.

2. The adjective in this construction denotes the resulting state or condition, as in 봄에는 날씨가 따뜻해져요 'In spring, the weather becomes warmer'. If a present state is a result of a change in the past, the past tense form is used, as in 이제 깨끗해졌어요 'It's now become clean'.

3. The following table shows the conjugation patterns.

ㅂ irregular	춥다	추워지다
	덥다	더워지다
으 irregular	바쁘다	바빠지다
	예쁘다	예뻐지다
ㄹ irregular	멀다	멀어지다
	길다	길어지다
르 irregular	빠르다	빨라지다
	다르다	달라지다
하다	깨끗하다	깨끗해지다

Exercises

1. Change the following sentences using ~어/아지다.

    (1) 동생이 (예쁘다).   <u>동생이 예뻐졌어요.</u>

    (2) 여름에는 낮이 (길다).   _____

    (3) 날씨가 (흐리다).   _____

    (4) 시험이 (어렵다).   _____

    (5) 기온이 (낮다).   _____

    (6) 시험이 끝나서 시간이 (많다). _____

    (7) 하늘이 (맑다).   _____

2. Give an appropriate response in the following situations.

    (1)   여름이 되었어요.   <u>날씨가 더워졌어요.</u>

    (2)   대학교 4학년이 되었어요.   _____

    (3)   친구를 오래간만에 만났어요. _____

    (4)   기온이 많이 내려갔어요.   _____

    (5)   구름이 많이 끼었어요.   _____

3. Using ~어/아질 거예요, make a prediction about the change of state resulting from the given situation.

    (1)   날씨가 더웠는데 비가 왔어요.

           <u>시원해질 거예요.</u>

    (2)   겨울이 되었어요.

           _____

    (3)   이번 학기에 외국어를 세 과목 들어요.

           _____

    (4)   학교가 너무 멀어서 이번 주말에 기숙사로 이사해요.

           _____

    (5)   여름이라서 사람들이 여행을 많이 해요.

           _____

G1.2	Sentence ending ~잖아요 'You know, . . .' (assuming agreement)

    (1) A: 오늘 야외에서 수업해요?

          B: 네, 날씨가 좋**잖아요**.

    (2) A: 토요일에 콘서트에 같이 갈래요?

          B: 저는 못 가요. 주말에 일하**잖아요**.

    (3) A: 방 공기가 차네요.

          B: 에어컨을 틀었**잖아요**.

    (4) A: 제니 씨가 이번 시험에 A+를 받았어요.

          B: 그동안 열심히 공부했**잖아요**.

Examples

Notes

1. This construction is used when the speaker assumes that the listener will agree with him/her. It is used when the speaker wants to reconfirm facts already known.

2. Although this form originated from a negative question (~지 않아요?), the intonation is not that of a question.

Exercises

1. Look at the pictures and provide an appropriate response.

(1)

A: 날씨가 추워졌어요.

B: <u>비가 오잖아요.</u>

(2)

A: 학생들이 밖에 나가고 싶어해요.

B: _____

(3)

A: 스티브 씨가 이번 주에 학교에 안 오네요.

B: _____

(4)

A: 리사가 한국어를 잘 하네요.

B: _____

(5)

A: 피곤한데 집에 택시 타고 갈까요?

B: _____

2. Give an appropriate response to the following statements.

   (1) (A and B have been working hard since early in the morning.)

       A: 배가 고프네요.

       B: <u>벌써 오후 2시잖아요. 스파게티 먹으러 가요</u>.

   (2) (A and B have been studying in the library for three hours.)

       A: 굉장히 피곤하네요.

       B: _____

   (3) (A calls his girlfriend long-distance every day.)

       A: 이번 달에 전화비가 많이 나왔어요.

       B: _____

   (4) (우진 and five of his friends went to a restaurant.)

       A: 음식값이 굉장히 많이 나왔네요.

       B: _____

   (5) (A and B know that Steve has been playing tennis since childhood.)

       A: 스티브 씨는 테니스를 참 잘 치네요.

       B: _____

Notes

CULTURE

음력과 양력   The use of the lunar and solar (Gregorian) calendars

한국에서는 양력[1]과 음력[2]을 다 씁니다.
옛날에는 음력만 썼지만 1896년부터 양력도
같이 쓰기 시작했습니다. 음력은 달[3]의 모양[4]이
바뀌는 것을 보고 만든 달력[5]입니다. 음력으로
한 달이 29일 또는 30일이 될 수도 있습니다.
옛날[6]부터 음력은 농사[7]와 어업[8]에 아주
중요했습니다.

한국의 국경일[9]들은 모두 양력을 씁니다.
그렇지만 아주 큰 명절[10]들은
(설날, 추석) 음력을 쓰고 있습니다. 그리고 생일에 음력을 쓰는 사람들이
많습니다. 그래서 보통 한국의 달력에는 양력 날짜와 음력 날짜[11]가 모두
있습니다.

The Lunar Calendar

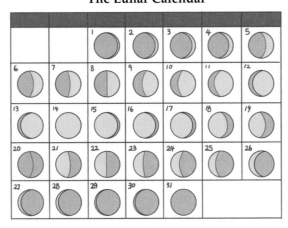

1. 양력: solar calendar
2. 음력: lunar calendar
3. 달: moon
4. 모양: shape
5. 달력: calendar
6. 옛날: the old days

7. 농사: farming
8. 어업: fishery
9. 국경일: national holidays
10. 명절: traditional holidays
11. 날짜: date

Conversation 2 | 날씨가 추워졌네요.

▶ 학교 앞에서 민지와 스티브가 만났습니다.

Conversation 2

민지: 오늘 참 춥지요?

스티브: 네, 따뜻하던^{G1.3} 날씨가 어젯밤부터 갑자기
         추워졌네요.

민지: 비가 온 다음에는 날씨가 추워지잖아요.
         스티브 씨, 아파트는 어때요? 따뜻해요?

스티브: 보통은 따뜻한데, 어젯밤에는 난방이
         안 돼서 굉장히 추웠어요.

민지: 어머, 그랬어요? 고생했겠네요.
         이번 주말엔 날씨가 따뜻했으면 좋겠어요.^{G1.4}

스티브: 참, 일요일에 잠실 운동장에서
         야구 시합이 있는데, 같이 안 갈래요?

민지: 아, 그럴까요?

스티브: 두꺼운 옷을 입고 오세요. 지난 번 야구장에
         갔을 때^{G1.5}는 바람이 너무 많이 불어서 혼났어요.

◗ COMPREHENSION QUESTIONS

1. 그동안 날씨가 어땠습니까?
2. 언제부터 갑자기 추워졌습니까?
3. 스티브는 왜 어젯밤에 춥게 잤습니까?
4. 어디에서 야구 시합을 합니까?
5. 야구장에 갈 때 왜 두꺼운 옷을 입고 가야 합니까?

◗ NEW WORDS

NOUN

고생(하다)	hardship
난방	heating
데이트(하다)	a date
도	degree
라디오	radio
물건	merchandise
바람	wind
섭씨	Celsius
시합	game, match
야구(하다)	baseball
야구장	baseball stadium
운동장	schoolyard, field
일기예보	weather forecast
잠실	Jamsil
프로	program
현재	the present

VERB

계속되다	to continue
불다	to blow
알리다	to inform
없어지다	to disappear
추워지다	to get colder
혼나다	to have a hard time
흐려지다	to get cloudy

ADJECTIVE

| 더럽다 | to be dirty |
| 두껍다 | to be thick |

ADVERB

갑자기	suddenly
꼭	surely, certainly
대체로	generally, mostly
먼저	first, beforehand

SUFFIX

~(으)ㄴ 때	
~(으)면 좋겠다	I wish
~던	used to

◗ NEW EXPRESSIONS

1. 난방이 안 되다 means 'the heating system does not work'. 되다 'to become' is one of the most common idiomatic verbs, as shown in the usages below.

봄이 되었다.	Spring has come.
오 년이 되었다.	It has been five years.
키가 육 피트가 됩니다.	He is six feet tall. (amount to)
밥이 잘 안 되었다.	The rice did not turn out very well. (result)
준비가 다 되었다.	It is ready.
비즈니스가 잘 됩니다.	Business is good.
인터넷이 안 돼요.	The Internet does not work.

2. 굉장히 means 'very, extremely, enormously'. Similar adverbs are 무척, 아주, 몹시, 참, and 되게 (colloquial).

3. 혼나다 means 'to get frightened out of one's wits, have a bitter experience, get scolded (by someone)'. In the text, the meaning is 'to have a hard time' or 'to suffer a lot'. Literally 혼 means 'the spirit' or 'the soul' and 나다 is 'to go out'.

Grammar

G1.3   Noun-modifying form ~던 (retrospective)

(1) A: 춥**던** 날씨가 갑자기 따뜻해졌어요.
          The weather, which had been cold, became cold suddenly.

    B: 네. 일기예보를 봤는데 현재 기온이 섭씨 20도나 돼요.
          Yes. The temperature has reached 20 degrees Celsius, according to the weather forecast.

(2) A: 재미있**던** 코미디 프로가 언제부터 없어졌어요?

    B: 지난 봄부터 없어졌어요.

(3) 크**던** 옷이 작아졌어요.

(4) A: 한국에 가면 뭐 하고 싶어요?

    B: 어렸을 때 살**던** 집에 가 보고 싶어요.

(5) 내가 전에 데이트하**던** 남자가 다른 여자와 사귀어요.

Examples

Notes

1. With the noun-modifying suffix ~던, the speaker describes an actual past situation (event or state) as if he/she were observing or perceiving it at the moment.

2. Often the meaning implies that the past situation does not exist any longer. When attached to an adjective stem, ~던 implies a change from the past state, as in (1) – (3).

3. When it is attached to a verb stem, on the other hand, it may mean a habitual action that did not continue. In this case, it renders the meaning of 'used to', as in (4) and (5).

Adjectives

~던	~(으)ㄴ	~(으)ㄹ
좋던	좋은	좋을
따뜻하던	따뜻한	따뜻할

(i) 좋던 날씨가 흐려졌어요.
The weather, which had been good, became cloudy.
(ii) 좋은 사람을 만났어요.
I met a nice person.
(iii) 내일 날씨가 좋을 거예요.
Tomorrow the weather will be nice.

Verbs

~던	~(으)ㄴ	~는	~(으)ㄹ
읽던 책	읽은 책	읽는 책	읽을 책
다니던 학교	다닌 학교	다니는 학교	다닐 학교

(i) 어제 읽던 책이 없어졌어요.
The book I was reading yesterday disappeared.
(ii) 이게 어제 읽은 책이에요?
Is this the book you read yesterday?
(iii) 지금 읽는 책 재미있어요?
Is the book you are reading now fun?
(iv) 내일 읽을 책이 많아요?
Do you have a lot of books to read tomorrow?

Exercises

1. Complete the following sentences.

(1) <u>하얗던</u> 눈이 더러워졌습니다.

(2) _____ 옷이 깨끗해졌습니다.

(3) _____ 날씨가 더워졌습니다.

(4) _____ 동생이 키가 커졌습니다.

(5) _____ 교통이 편리해졌습니다.

(6) _____ 아버지가 시간이 많아지셨습니다.

2. Translate the following sentences.

(1) This is the restaurant I used to go to often last year.

_____

(2) The TV program I used to watch nine years ago was *Dooly*.

_____

(3) Boston is a place where I used to live eleven years ago.

_____

G1.4	Expressing speaker's wish: ~(으)면 좋겠다

Examples

(1) A: 요즘 많이 춥지요?

B: 네, 빨리 봄이 **오면 좋겠어요**.

(2) A: 돈이 많**으면 좋겠어요**.

B: 돈이 많으면 뭐 하고 싶은데요?

A: 집을 꼭 사고 싶어요.

(3) A: 밤에 영화 볼래요?

B: 피곤해서 잤**으면 좋겠어요**.

(4) A: 날씨가 너무 덥네요.

B: 바람 좀 불었**으면 좋겠지요?**

Notes

This construction ~(으)면 좋겠어요 means "It'd be nice if . . . were the case"
but can be translated as "I wish . . ." The meaning of strong wish is expressed
when the past-tense marker is used with ~(으)면, as in 친구가 빨리 왔으면
좋겠어요.

Exercises

1. Answer the following questions, using ~(으)면 좋겠어요.

(1) 내일 뭐 하고 싶어요? (등산가다)
 등산 갔으면 좋겠어요.

(2) 어젯밤에 잘 못 잤어요? (지금 쉬다)
 _____

(3) 시장에 가야 해요? (좋은 물건을 싸게 사다)
 _____

(4) 유럽에 가 봤어요? (가 보다)
 _____

(5) 친구하고 영화 보러 가요? (재미있다)
 _____

(6) 한국에서 뭘 할 거예요? (한국어를 공부하다)
 _____

2. What would you wish in the following situations? Answer in Korean.

(1) The soup is too salty.
(2) You just found out that there is an exam tomorrow.
(3) Your credit card has reached its limit.
(4) You need to call home, but you cannot find a phone nearby.

G1.5   N 때 'at the time of N'; ~(으)ㄹ 때 'when'

(1)   중학교 **때** 무슨 과목이 제일 재미있었어요?

(2)   A: 초등학교 **때** 어디서 살았어요?
       B: 열살 **때**까지 서울에서 살았어요.

(3)   A: **공부할 때** 음악을 들으세요?   Do you listen to music
                                                          when you study?

       B: 저는 **공부할 때** 다른 일을   When I study, I can't do
              못 해요.   other things.

(4)   A: **시간 있을 때** 뭐 해요?
       B: 컴퓨터 게임도 하고 음악도 들어요.

(5)   **한국에서 살았을 때** 제주도(Cheju Island)에 가 봤어요.

Notes

1. [Noun 때] refers to the duration of the event, activity, or process denoted by the noun. Nouns that do not themselves indicate time may be followed by 때 as in 올림픽('Olympic Game') 때 and 시험 때. However, time-indicating expressions such as 아침, 주말, and 작년 are combined with the temporal particle 에 instead as in 아침에, 주말에, 작년에, 밤에, 일월에, 가을에.

   For some expressions such as 아침, 점심, 저녁, and 방학, both 때 and 에 can be used. 아침 때 means 'at the time of morning/breakfast' whereas 아침에 means 'in the morning'.

2. ~(으)ㄹ 때 is used with a verb or an adjective when two events overlap in time. For example, in (3A), the event of "studying" and the event of "listening to music" overlap. ~때 is used with a noun as in examples (1) and (2).

Additional grammar points: Although ~(으)면 (G1.4) also means 'when' (in addition to its conditional meaning), ~(으)면 and ~(으)ㄹ 때 differ. ~(으)ㄹ 때 deals only with time; ~(으)면 expresses an inherent relationship between the two clauses. For example, 겨울이 될 때 눈이 와요 is less natural here than 겨울이 되면 눈이 와요 because there is a close relationship between the season and the weather, and thus the second is preferred.

Exercises

1. Fill in the blanks with either 때 or 에.

    (1)   방학 때   (2)   주말_____

    (3)   학기말_____   (4)   대학교_____

    (5)   봄_____   (6)   시험_____

2. Change the verbs or adjectives in parentheses to show that the two events/activities/processes are concurrent.

    (1) (스키 타다) 때 조심하세요.

        <u>스키 탈 때 조심하세요.</u>

    (2) (숙제하다) 때 음악을 들어요?

        _____

    (3) 돈이 (없다) 때 친구한테 전화를 해요.

        _____

    (4) 처음 대학교에 (오다) 때 친구가 한 명도 없었어요.

        _____

    (5) 날씨가 (춥다) 때 스웨터를 자주 입어요.

        _____

    (6) 대답을 (모르다) 때 선생님께 질문해요.

        _____

    (7) 콘서트에 (가다) 때 무슨 옷을 입어요?

        _____

3. Ask your partner these questions and report the responses to your class.

(1) 시험 때 몇 시까지 공부해요?

_____

(2) 지난 봄 방학 때 뭐 했어요?

_____

(3) 이번 여름 방학 때 뭐 할 거예요?

_____

(4) 학교에 올 때 누구하고 같이 와요?

_____

(5) 어렸을 때 어디에서 살았어요?

_____

(6) 고등학교 다닐 때 무슨 운동 좋아했어요?

_____

Narration　　　일기 예보

안녕하십니까? 오늘의 날씨를 알려
드리겠습니다. 아침에는 따뜻하고
맑겠지만 낮부터는 흐려져서
구름이 많이 끼겠고 저녁 때는 비가
오기 시작하겠습니다. 오늘 아침
기온은 섭씨 6도,
낮 기온은 13도가 되겠습니다. 내일 아침 기온은 오늘보다
낮아지고 찬 바람이 불겠습니다. 낮부터 맑아져서 서울은
주말까지 대체로 좋은 날씨가 계속되겠습니다. 서울의 현재
기온은 9도입니다. 감기 조심하십시오.

▶▶ COMPREHENSION QUESTIONS

1. 오늘 아침 날씨는 어떻습니까?
2. 언제부터 비가 오기 시작합니까?
3. 내일 아침에는 오늘 아침보다 더 따뜻해집니까?
4. 서울의 주말 날씨는 어떻습니까?

NEW EXPRESSIONS

1. Some of the common terms used in 일기예보 'weather forecast' are:

맑다	to be clear
흐리다	to be cloudy
구름이 끼다	to get cloudy
비가 오다	to rain
눈이 오다	to snow
바람이 불다	the wind blows

2. Change of temperature (기온) is expressed by 낮아지다 and 높아지다. A degree (도) of temperature is indicated exclusively by 섭씨 'Celsius' and not by 화씨 'Fahrenheit' in Korea.

기온이 낮아진다.   The temperature goes down.
기온이 높아진다.   The temperature goes up.

$C = (F - 32) \times 5/9$ $F = C \times 9/5 + 32$

섭씨 C	−10°	0°	10°	20°	30°	36.5°	100°
화씨 F	14°	32°	50°	68°	83°	97.7°	212°

3. 알리다 'to inform, announce' is often used with the benefactive auxiliary verb 드리다 or 주다 'to do for', as in:

선생님께 이 뉴스를   We have to inform the teacher of
알려 드려야 해요.   this news (for him/her).
내일까지 알려 주세요.   Inform me by tomorrow (for me).

4. 계속하다 'to continue something' is a transitive verb (a verb taking an object) while 계속되다 'something continues' is an intransitive verb (a verb without an object).

수업을 계속했습니다.   (The teacher) continued the class.
수업이 계속되었습니다.   The class continued.

USAGE

1 *Describing weather*

(1) 성희: 오늘 날씨 참 좋지요?
마크: 네, 정말 좋은데요.
성희 씨는 어느 계절을 제일 좋아하세요?
성희: 저는 가을이 제일 좋아요.
날씨도 시원해지고 공기도 깨끗하잖아요.
마크 씨는 어느 계절이 좋으세요?
마크: 저는 스키도 탈 수 있고 방학도 길어서 겨울이 더
좋아요.

(2) A: 오늘 날씨가 어때요?
B: 공기가 맑고 시원해요.
A: 어제 날씨는 어땠어요?
B: 바람이 불고 추웠어요.
A: 날씨가 좋으면 이번 주말에 뭐 하고 싶으세요?
B: 바닷가에 수영하러 갔으면 좋겠어요.

Useful expressions

봄: 따뜻한 날씨
꽃이 피는 날씨 (the weather when flowers bloom)
맑은 날씨

여름: 더운 날씨
갑자기 비가 오는 날씨
무더운 날씨 (hot and humid weather)
장마 (the summer rainy season)

가을: 시원한 날씨
쌀쌀한 날씨 (chilly weather)
단풍이 들다 (to put on the tints of autumn foliage)

겨울: 눈이 오는 날씨
얼음이 얼다 (ice forms)
흐린 날씨
공기가 건조하다 (dry air)

Exercise 1

Ask your partner the following questions and report the result to the class.

(1) 어느 계절을 제일 좋아하세요? 왜요?

(2) 흐리고 비가 오는 날에는 보통 뭐 하는 걸 좋아하세요?

(3) 이번 주말에 날씨가 좋으면 뭐 하고 싶으세요?

(4) 날씨가 추운 날/비가 오는 날/눈이 오는 날/바람이 많이

부는 날 무슨 옷을 입으세요?

Exercise 2

Report the four seasons where you live and say what effect the weather has on you.

Exercise 3

Read the following weather map of Korea and answer the questions.

(1) 서울에 비가 올까요?

(2) 어느 곳이 제일 시원할까요?

(3) 서울과 부산은 어디가 더 덥습니까?

(4) 해가 지는 시간은 어떻게 됩니까? (해 지는 시간 sunset)

(5) 달이 뜨는 시간은 어떻게 됩니까? (달 뜨는 시간 moonrise)

(6) 지금은 겨울입니까? 봄입니까?

(7) 제주도의 날씨는 어떻습니까?

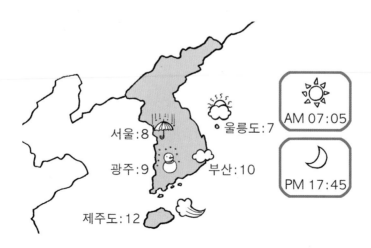

서울:8
울릉도:7
광주:9
부산:10
제주도:12

AM 07:05

PM 17:45

2 *Indicating possibility and capability*

Examples

(1) A: 날씨가 좋으면 밖에서 무슨 운동을 할 수 있어요?
   B: 테니스도 칠 수 있고 골프도 칠 수 있어요.
   A: 날씨가 추울 때는 무슨 운동을 할 수 있어요?
   B: 스키도 탈 수 있고 농구(basketball)도 할 수 있어요.

(2) A: 테니스 칠 줄 아세요?
   B: 네, 배웠는데 잘 못 쳐요.

(3) A: 한국어를 컴퓨터로 칠 줄 아세요?
   B: 네, 할 수 있어요.

Exercise 1

무엇을 할 줄 아세요? Converse with your partner about three items in each given category about what you can do. When you have finished, change partners.

	1	2	3
노래			
외국어			
운동			
요리			

Exercise 2

What can you do under the following weather conditions?

(1) 비 오는 날:

(2) 바람 부는 날:

(3) 눈 오는 날:

(4) 추운 날:

(5) 더운 날:

3   *Listening to weather forecasts*

(1)   Narration

안녕하십니까? 오늘 날씨를 알려 드리겠습니다. 아침에는 따뜻하고
맑겠지만 낮부터는 흐려져서 구름이 많이 끼겠고 저녁때는 비가
오기 시작하겠습니다. 오늘 아침 기온은 섭씨 6도, 낮 기온은 13도가
되겠습니다. 내일은 낮부터 맑아져서 서울은 주말까지 좋은 날씨가
계속되겠습니다. 내일은 아침 기온은 오늘보다 낮아지고 찬바람이
불겠습니다. 감기 조심하십시오.

(2)   텔레비전 일기예보

내일 아침 서울 지방은 기온이 영하 5도까지 떨어지는 다소 추운 날씨가
되겠습니다. 하지만 낮부터 기온이 올라가면서 비교적 포근하겠습니다.
이번 달은 맑고 건조한 날씨가 계속되겠습니다.

(change of screen)

각 지방의 내일 날씨입니다. 중부 지방은 대체로 맑겠습니다. 강원, 영서
지방은 아침에 안개 끼는 곳이 있겠습니다. 남부와 제주도 지방은 오전에
흐리다가 오후부터 차차 맑아지겠습니다. 아침 최저 기온은 오늘보다
낮겠지만 낮 최고 기온은 오늘보다 높아져 포근하겠습니다.

▶ **Useful words**

각 each, 기온 temperature, 영하 below the freezing point, 다소 more or less/
to some degree, 비교적 relatively, 포근하다 to be warm, 건조한 dry, 화면
a (television) screen, 지방 region, 중부 지방 the central districts, 대체로
generally, 맑다 to be clear, 강원 Gangwon region, 영서 Youngseo region,
안개 끼다 to be foggy, 남부 southern, 차차 gradually, 최저 the lowest, 최고 the
highest

Exercise 1

Use the weather forecast (1) above and converse with another student as in the example.

Example: Student 1: 오늘 낮 날씨는 어때요?
Student 2: 흐리고 구름이 많이 낄 거예요.

Exercise 2

Based on the weather forecast (2) above, answer the following questions.

(1) 내일 아침 서울의 오전과 오후 날씨는 어떻습니까?

(2) 이번 달의 날씨는 어떻습니까?

(3) 내일 아침 안개가 끼는 곳은 어느 지방입니까?

(4) 내일 남부 지방과 제주도의 오전 날씨는 어떻습니까?

Exercise 3

Listen to the weather forecast announcement made by your teacher and answer questions.

Exercise 4

Find a weather forecast for your town in the newspaper and report it to the class in Korean.

Lesson 1 Weather and Seasons

CONVERSATION 1   *Which season do you like most?*

▶ Minji and Mark are talking in front of the library.

Minji: The weather has become a lot cooler, hasn't it?

Mark: Yes, it has become very cool. The summer has finished and it has already become autumn. This summer was boring because the rainy season lasted unusually long.

Minji: Mark, which season do you like most?

Mark: I like spring the most. You know, because the weather is warm and the flowers bloom a lot. How about you, Minji?

Minji: I like winter better because I can ski and, also, the school vacation is long.

Mark: Do you? Then, you must long for the winter, Minji.

Minji: Yes, but I also like autumn because I can see the autumn foliage. By the way, Mark, I will go to Seorak Mount in October to see the autumn foliage. Do you want to go with me?

Mark: To see the autumn foliage? I wanted to see it even before you mentioned it, so it works out well.

CONVERSATION 2   *The weather has become cold.*

▶ Minji and Steve meet in front of the school.

Minji: Steve, how are you? Today it is very cold, isn't it? The weather was warm but has suddenly become colder since last night.

Steve: You know, the weather becomes colder after rain.

Minji: Is your apartment warm?

Steve: It is usually warm, but last night the heating didn't work, so it was very cold.

Minji: Oh, was it? You must have had a hard time. It will be nice if it is warm this weekend.

Steve: By the way, there is a baseball game at Jamsil Stadium this weekend. Will you go with me?

Minji: Oh, should I?

Steve: Wear thick clothes. The last time I went to the baseball stadium, I had a hard time because the wind made it cold.

NARRATION   *Today's weather*

How are you? Let me announce today's weather. In the morning, it will be warm and clear. However, at noon it will become overcast, so there will be many clouds in the sky. In the evening it will begin to rain. This morning's temperature is 6 degrees Celsius. The daytime temperature will rise to 13 degrees Celsius. Tomorrow morning's temperature will be lower than today's, and there will be a cold wind blowing. The sky will become clearer throughout the day, and Seoul will have mostly good weather until the weekend. The current temperature in Seoul is 9 degrees. Watch out for the cold.

CULTURE   *Lunar and solar calendars*

People use both the lunar and solar (Gregorian) calendars in Korea. A long time ago, they used only the lunar calendar, but since 1896 they have used the solar (Gregorian) calendar as well. The lunar calendar follows the phases of the moon. One month can be either twenty-nine days or thirty days by the lunar calendar. It was very important in agriculture and fishing long ago.

All the Korean national holidays follow the solar calendar. However, some traditional holidays (New Year's Day, Thanksgiving Day) follow the lunar calendar. And many people follow the lunar calendar for their birthdays. Therefore, Korean calendars usually have both solar and lunar dates.

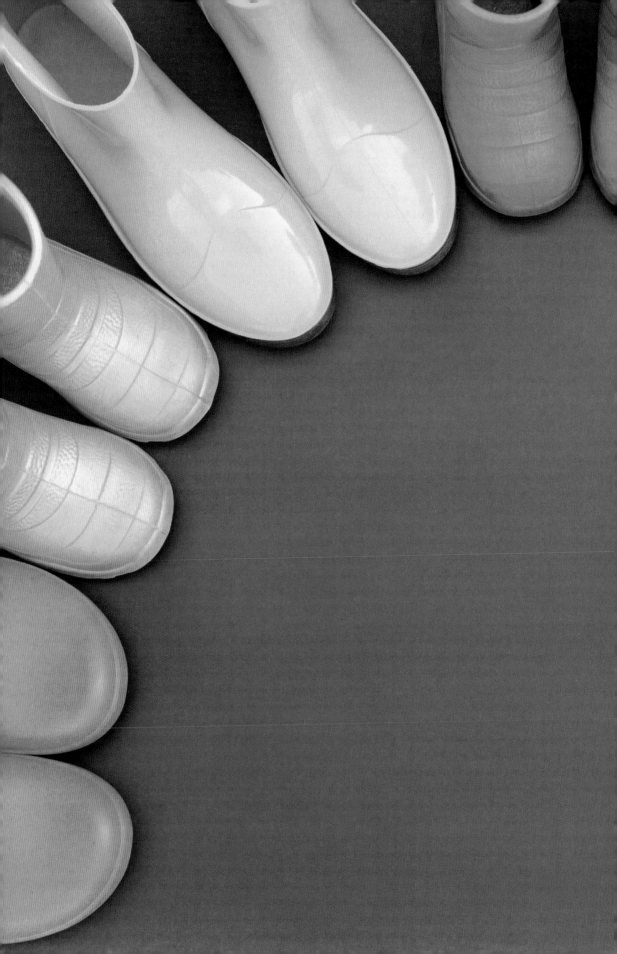

2과 옷과 유행

Lesson 2 Clothing and Fashion

Conversation 1   백화점에서 옷을 사려고 해요.

▶ 수빈이 민지에게 전화를 합니다.

Conversation   1

수빈: 민지 씨, 지금 백화점에서 세일하는데
        같이 안 갈래요?

민지: 마침 잘 됐네요. 저도 정장 한 벌을 사야 돼요.
        수빈씨는 뭐 살 거예요?

수빈: 저는 원피스하고 구두를 하나 사려고요.G2.1
        요즘 입을 옷이 없어서요.

민지: 저도 그래요. 한국은 옷 입는 스타일이
        캐나다하고 달라서 옷 입기가 어렵네요.G2.2

수빈: 민지 씨는 어떤 정장이 필요하세요?

민지: 인터뷰할 때 입을 단정한 치마 정장이 필요해요.

COMPREHENSION QUESTIONS

1. 수빈이는 백화점에서 무엇을 사려고 합니까?
2. 왜 한국에서는 옷 입기가 어렵습니까?
3. 민지는 어떤 정장을 사려고 합니까?

NEW WORDS

NOUN

구두	dress shoes
굽	heel
단어	vocabulary
마음	mind, heart
반값	half price
반바지	shorts
블라우스	blouse
샌들	sandals
스타일	style
원피스	(one-piece) dress
유행(하다)	fashion, trend
자켓	jacket
정가	regular price
정장	suit, formal dress
치마	skirt
카메라	camera
현금	cash

COUNTER

벌	a pair of (counter)

VERB

닫다	to close
(나이가) 들다	to gain age
(마음에) 들다	to be to one's liking
떠나다	to leave
(돈을) 벌다	to earn (money)
외우다	to memorize

ADJECTIVE

높다	to be high
단정하다	to be neat
얇다	to be thin
필요하다	to be necessary

ADVERB

마침	just, just in time
아직도	yet, still
함께	together, along with

SUFFIX

~(으)려고 하다	intend to
~기가 쉽다/ 어렵다	it is easy/ difficult to . . .

NEW EXPRESSIONS

1. 세일, 바겐 세일 'a bargain sale'

백화점에서 세일을 해요.	There is a sale in the department store.
이 옷은 세일이에요.	These clothes are on sale.

2. 마침 'coincidentally, as it just happens'
   친구한테 전화를 하려고 했는데 마침 친구한테서 전화가 왔어요.
   마침 돈이 있어서 필요한 책을 살 수 있었어요.

   A: 저 지금 우체국에 가는데 필요한 거 있으면 말씀하세요.
   B: 마침 잘 됐네요. 우표 좀 사다 주세요.

3. 바지 한 벌 'one pair of pants', 옷 한 벌 'one suit', 투피스 세 벌 'three women's suits', 양복 두 벌 'two men's suits', 청바지 네 벌 'four pairs of blue jeans'.

4. 필요하다 'to need, be necessary' is an adjective, unlike the English verb "need". Thus, it is used with the particle 이/가, as in 책이 필요합니다, not 책을 필요합니다.

Grammar

G2.1   V.S.~(으)려고 'intending to'; V.S.~(으)려고 하다 'intend to'

[~(으)려고]
(1) A: 어디 가세요?
     B: 얇은 자켓하고 반바지 사**려고** 백화점에 가요.

(2) A: 뭐 하**려고** 은행에서 현금을 찾았어요?
     B: 친구와 함께 여행 가고 싶어서요.

(3) A: 왜 경제학을 공부해요?
     B: 돈을 많이 벌**려고요**.

[~(으)려고 하다]
(4) A: 오늘 카메라 안 사세요?
     B: 크리스마스 세일할 때 반값에 사**려고요**.
     A: 정가가 얼마인데요?
     B: 300,000원이요.

(5) A: 비가 오**려고 하네요**.
     B: 어제부터 날씨가 흐렸지요?

(6) A: 세일 때 뭐 좀 샀어요?
     B: 청바지 하나 사**려고** 했는데 바빠서 못 갔어요.

(7) A: 오늘도 늦게 잘 거예요?
     B: 오늘은 피곤해서 일찍 자**려고요**.

Examples

Notes

1. **~(으)려고** is mainly used to express the speaker's intention or plan. It also has the meaning of 'being about to', in addition to 'in an effort to' and 'intending to'.

> 건강해지려고 매일 운동합니다. (in an effort to)
> 신문을 읽으려고 샀습니다. (intending to)
> 성희는 일찍 자려고 합니다. (plan)
> 버스가 떠나려고 합니다. (be about to)

2. Unlike **~(으)러**, which is followed only by a verb of going and coming, there is no such constraint with **~(으)려고**.

> 옷을 한 벌 사**러** 백화점에 갔어요.
> 옷을 한 벌 사**려고** 백화점에 갔어요.
> 공부를 하**려고** 책을 한 권 샀어요.
> 공부를 하**러** 책을 한 권 샀어요. (X)

3. In colloquial speech, **~(으)ㄹ라(구) 그래요** or **~(으)ㄹ라구 해요** is often used instead of **~(으)려고 해요**. Also, the verb **하다** can be omitted from the suffix **~(으)려고 (해)요** as in (7).

Exercises

1. Using ~(으)려고, answer the following questions.

(1) A: 웬일이세요?
B: <u>사전 좀 빌리려고 전화했어요.</u>

(2) A: 왜 한국말을 공부해요?
B: _____

(3) A: 왜 은행에서 돈을 많이 찾았어요(withdraw money)?
B: _____

(4) A: 왜 이 식당에 자주 와요?
B: _____

(5) A: 왜 한국에 왔어요?
B: _____

2. Using ~(으)려고 하다, ask your partner what he/she plans to do in the following situations.

(1) A: 여름 방학에 뭐 하려고 하세요?

B: 많이 쉬고 싶어요. 그리고 여행도 하려고 해요.

(2) A: 이번 주말에 _____

B: _____

(3) A: 오늘밤 자기 전에 _____

B: _____

(4) A: 다음 주 여행 떠나기 전에 _____

B: _____

G2.2   V.S.~기(가) 쉽다/어렵다 'it is easy/difficult to . . .'

(1) A: 한국에서 옷 입기가 어때요?

B: 미국하고 스타일이 달라서 옷 **입기가 참 어려워요**.

(2) A: 아직도 블라우스 못 샀어요?

B: 네, 마음에 드는 걸 찾**기가 어렵네요**.

(3) A: 어디가 불편하세요?

B: 샌들 굽이 높아서 걷**기가 힘들어요**.

Notes

1. ~기(가) 쉽다/어렵다 is used to comment on how easy or difficult it is to do a certain action.

2. Other adjectives may be used to comment on other aspects of the action:

~기(가) 힘들다	it is difficult to . . .
~기(가) 좋다	it is easy/convenient to use for . . .
~기(가) 편하다/불편하다	it is convenient/inconvenient to . . .
~기(가) 싫다	I don't want to . . .

나이가 들면 단어 외우는 것이 힘들어요.
서울에서는 지하철 타기가 편리해요.

3. Compare ~기(가) 좋다 with ~는 것이/게 좋다. ~는 것이/게 좋다 means 'doing . . . is good for you' or 'you'd better do . . . ,' while 하기 좋다 means 'it is convenient . . . '

　　　어렸을 때 외국어 공부를 열심히 하는 게 좋아요.

Exercises

1. Give a few examples that belong to each category.

　　(1) 쓰기 쉬운 컴퓨터: _____

　　(2) 읽기 어려운 책: _____

　　(3) 먹기 싫은 음식: _____

　　(4) 운전하기 좋은 차: _____

　　(5) 듣기 좋은 음악: _____

　　(6) 신기 편한 신발: _____

　　(7) 하기 쉬운 운동: _____

　　(8) 살기 불편한 곳: _____

2. Complete the following sentences using ~기 어렵다/힘들다/쉽다/편하다/불편하다/좋다/싫다.

　　(1) 일요일 밤에 파티를 자주 해요. 그래서 <u>월요일에는 일찍</u>

　　　　<u>일어나기가 힘들어요</u>.

　　(2) 밖이 시끄러워요. 그래서 _____

　　(3) 책값이 비싸요. 그래서 _____

　　(4) 주말에는 길이 많이 막혀요. 그래서 _____

　　　　_____

　　(5) 늦은 밤에는 식당을 다 닫아요. 그래서 _____

　　　　_____

　　(6) 새로 산 구두가 너무 작아요. 그래서 _____

　　　　_____

Conversation 2   날씨가 추워졌네요.

▌ 수빈이와 민지는 옷을 사러 백화점에 갔습니다

Conversation   2

점원: 어서 오세요. 어떤 옷을 찾으세요?

수빈: 구경 좀 하려고요.

점원: 네, 천천히 골라 보세요.

수빈: 저기, 요즘 어떤 치마가 유행이에요?

점원: 요즘 짧은 치마가 유행인데 이거 어떠세요?

수빈: 초록색 말고[G2.3] 남색은 없어요?

점원: 요즘은 어두운 색보다 밝은 색이 인기가
         많아요. 노란색이나 하늘색은 어떠세요?

수빈: 그러면 둘 다 입어 봐도 돼요?[G2.4]

점원: 네, 그럼요.

         (입어 보고 나서)

수빈: 민지 씨, 저한테 어떤 색이 어울려요?

민지: 수빈 씨한테는 하늘색이 더 잘 어울리는 것
         같아요.[G2.5]

수빈: 그래요? (점원에게) 그럼 하늘색으로 주세요.

COMPREHENSION QUESTIONS

1. 수빈이는 무슨 옷을 사고 싶어합니까?
2. 수빈이는 무슨 옷을 입어 봤습니까?
3. 요즘 어떤 옷이 유행입니까?
4. 요즘 어떤 색이 인기가 많습니까?
5. 수빈이한테는 어떤 색이 잘 어울립니까?

NEW WORDS

NOUN

가격	price
검정색	black
남색	navy blue, indigo
노란색	yellow
담배	cigarette
문제	problem
빨간색	red
(신용) 카드	credit card
와이셔츠	dress shirt
인기	popularity
점퍼	jumper, jacket
초록색	green
티셔츠	T-shirt
파란색	blue
하늘색	sky blue
흰색	white

CONJUNCTIVE

그러면	then, in that case

VERB

뛰다	to run
맞다	to fit
모자라다	to lack
바꾸다	to change
어울리다	to match, suit
피우다	to smoke

ADJECTIVE

밝다	to be bright
어둡다	to be dark

ADVERB

말고	not . . . but . . .
천천히	slowly

PARTICLE

(으)로	item selected from among many

SUFFIX

~(으)ㄴ/는/(으)ㄹ 것 같다	it seems like
~어/아도 되다	expresses permission

NEW EXPRESSIONS

1. While 유행 'fashion' is a noun, 유행하다 'to be in fashion, be in vogue' is a verb. So, the modifier form is 유행하는, as in 유행하는 옷, 유행하는 음악.

2. 유행하다 is an adjective meaning 'to be in fashion' while 유행이다 is a verb, though the meaning is similar.

> 긴 치마가 유행입니다. Long skirts are in fashion.
> 긴 치마가 유행합니다. Long skirts are in fashion.

The modifier forms are different because one is an adjective and the other is a verb as in

> 요즘 유행인 헤어스타일
> 요즘 유행하는 헤어스타일

3. 고르다 'to choose, select' is a 르-irregular verb, as in 골라요, 골라 주세요, 골랐어요, but 고르면, 고르세요.

4. 그럼 is a shortened form of the conjunctive 그러면/그렇다면 'then'.
In discourse, 그럼요 is also used as 'I agree with you totally'.

5. 어울리다 'to look good (on), go well (with)' is used with the particle 한테 or 에게.

> 빨간색이 수미한테 잘 어울려요.
> Red looks good on Sumi.

Grammar

G2.3   N1 말고 N2 'not N1 but N2'

Examples

(1) A: 이 초록색 점퍼 어떠세요?
    B: 초록색 **말고** 빨간색으로 바꿔 주세요.

(2) A: 뉴스를 보고 싶은데요.
    B: 뉴스 **말고** 드라마를 보세요.

(3) A: 육개장 드릴까요?
    B: 저는 육개장 **말고** 불고기를 시키려고 해요.

(4) A: 이 원피스 어떠세요?
    B: 원피스 **말고** 바지 입어 볼게요.

Notes

1. When you choose one option over the other, 말고 is used after the first noun as shown above. Notice that it is normally used in command and proposal.

> 다음 학기에는 중국어 말고 한국어를 공부하세요.
> 티셔츠 말고 와이셔츠를 입는 게 어때요?

2. When an action is involved, a verb form is used, as in V.S.~지 말고.

> 내일이 시험이에요. 놀지 말고 공부하세요.
> 수업을 9시에 시작하지 말고 10시에 시작할까요?
> 도서관에서는 전화하지 말고 공부만 하세요.

Exercises

1. Give an alternative.

(1) A: 지금 숙제할까요?

B: <u>지금 말고 오후에 하면 어때요?</u>

How about doing it in the afternoon instead of now?

(2) A: 청소할까요?

B: _____

(3) A: 콘택트 렌즈(contact lens)를 낄까요?

B: _____

(4) A: 한국어를 전공할까요?

B: _____

(5) A: 저녁에 불고기를 먹을까요?

B: _____

(6) A: 흰색 점퍼를 살까요, 검정색 자켓을 살까요?

B: _____

2. Look at the pictures and suggest an item to your partner. Add a reason for your suggestion.

(1)  아이스크림 말고 콜라를 드세요.
돈이 모자라잖아요.

(2) _____

(3)  _____

(4) _____

G2.4   Expressions of permission and prohibition:
V.S.~어도/아도 되다; V.S.~(으)면 안 되다

(1) A: 식당에서 담배 피**워도 돼요**?   Would it be okay to smoke at a restaurant?

B: 아니요, 피우**면 안 돼요**.   No, it is not.

(2) A: 현금이 모자라는데 카드로 내**도 돼요**?   Can I pay with my card since I'm short of cash?

B: 네, 그럼요.   Yes, of course.

(3) A: 단어 시험 볼 때 점심 먹**어도 될까요**?

B: 아니요, 교실에서 먹**으면 안 돼요**.

(4) A: 파티에 정장 입고 가야 돼요?

B: 아니요, 정장 안 입**어도 돼요**/입**지 않아도 돼요**.

Notes

1. ~어도/아도 means 'even though, even if'. ~어도/아도 되다, literally meaning 'even though/if . . . , it is all right', is used to ask or grant permission. The negative form of ~어도/아도 되다 is 안 ~어도/아도 되다 or ~지 않아도 되다, as in (4).

괜찮다 'to be all right' or 좋다 'to be good' may be used instead of 되다 to be more specific with the meaning of permission.

2. ~(으)면 안 되다, literally meaning 'it is not all right, if . . .', is used to deny permission, prohibit a certain action, or give a warning.

Exercises

1. Provide an appropriate response in the given context.

(1) [수업이 끝났습니다.]
    학생: 지금 집에 가도 돼요?
    선생님: 네, 가도 돼요. or 아니요, 지금 가면 안 돼요.

(2) [학생이 교수님 연구실에 갔는데, 다른 학생이 벌써 있었습니다.]
    학생: 교수님, 밖에서 기다릴까요?
    교수님: 아니요, 괜찮아요. _____

(3) 학생: 선생님 오늘 숙제 내야 돼요?
    선생님: 아니요, _____
              그렇지만 내일까지는 내야 돼요.

(4) A: 수업 시간에 점심을 먹어도 돼요?
    B: _____

(5) A: 이 전화 좀 써도 돼요?
    B: _____

2. Ask permission appropriately in the given context.

(1) [In a shoe store]

A: <u>신발 좀 구경해도 돼요?</u>

B: 그럼요. 천천히 구경하세요.

(2) [B is going to treat A in a restaurant. A wants to check if B has enough money.]

A: _____?

B: 먹고 싶은 거 시키세요.
       그렇지만 너무 비싼 건 시키지 마세요.

(3) [A needs to make an emergency call, so A goes into a store.]

A: _____?

B: 네, 쓰세요. 전화 여기 있어요.

(4) [A and B have an appointment at B's office, and A wants to come now.]

A: _____?

B: 네, 오세요.

(5) [Steve visits a professor.]

스티브: _____?

교수님: 잠깐만 기다리세요.

Notes

. . . .

. . . .

. . . .

G2.5 ~(으)ㄴ/는/(으)ㄹ 것 같다 'it seems/looks like'

(1) 이 정장이 가격은 좀 비싸지만 저한테 잘 **맞는 것 같아요.**

(2) A: 새로 산 구두 굽이 너무 **높은 것 같아요.**
    B: 그래요? 한번 신어 보세요.

(3) A: 친구가 전화를 안 받아요.
    B: **여행 간 것 같아요.**

(4) A: 내일부터 추워**질 것 같지요?**
    B: 네, 눈도 **올 것 같아요.**

(5) A: 미나 씨가 노래를 정말 잘하지요?
    B: 네, 가수 **같아요.**

 Notes

1. ~(으)ㄴ/는/(으)ㄹ 것 같다 is an expression of resemblance or approximation. Even when the speaker has no doubt, it is quite common to use this pattern, as an indirect, thus more polite, way of expression.

	Verb	Adjective
Past	어젯밤에 잘 잔 것 같아요.	시험이 쉬웠던 것 같아요.
Present	지금 잘 자는 것 같아요.	시험이 쉬운 것 같아요.
Future	오늘 밤에는 잘 잘 것 같아요.	시험이 쉬울 것 같아요.

2. Noun + 같다 'It looks like [noun]'.

파란색 옷을 입은 분이 선생님 같아요.
재미있는 영화 같은데요.
저기에 옷이 많은 것 같은데, 들어가 볼까요?

3. 같아요 is often pronounced as [같애요].
. . . 것 같다 becomes [. . . 거 같다] in colloquial speech.

Exercises

1. Look at the following pictures and make observations.

(1)   밑이 추운 것 같아요.

(2)    피곤한 것 같아요

(3)   먹이운 는 거 같아요

(4)   _____

(5) _____

(6) _____

2. Respond to the following statements, using ~(으)ㄴ/는/(으)ㄹ 것 같다.

(1) 내일 날씨가 어떨까요?

_____

(2) 시험 문제가 어려울까요?

_____

(3) 빨간색이 저한테 잘 어울릴까요?

_____

(4) 밖에서 좀 뛰고 싶은데 날씨가 어때요?

_____

(5) 요즘 부모님 건강이 어떠세요?

_____

(6) 요즘 책 값이 어떤 것 같아요?

_____

(7) 어젯밤에 날씨가 어땠어요?

_____

(8) 요즘 서울 물가가 많이 올랐어요?

_____

Narration   백화점 쇼핑

오늘 수빈이는 친구 민지와 같이 옷을 사러 백화점에 갔습니다. 백화점 안은 쇼핑하러 온 사람들 때문에 아주 복잡했습니다. 수빈이는 요즘 유행하는 짧은 치마와 블라우스, 그리고 굽이 높은 샌들을 사고 민지는 운동할 때 입을 편한 바지와 티셔츠를 샀습니다. 한국은 유행이 자주 바뀌어서 옷 사기가 어렵습니다. 민지는 캐나다에 계시는 아버지께 드리려고 얇은 면 자켓도 하나 샀습니다. 세일을 해서 반값으로 싸게 살 수 있었습니다. 그런데 현금이 모자라서 카드로 냈습니다. 수빈이하고 민지는 마음에 꼭 드는 옷을 싸게 사서 기분이 아주 좋았습니다.

▶ COMPREHENSION QUESTIONS

1. 백화점이 왜 복잡했습니까?
2. 수빈이가 산 물건들을 다 써 보세요.
3. 민지는 어떤 자켓을 골랐습니까?
4. 민지는 왜 카드로 냈습니까?
5. 수빈이는 왜 기분이 좋았습니까?

NEW EXPRESSIONS

(1) The verb 계시다 is the honorific version of the verb 있다 'to be, stay'. It could be used as a main verb as in (a) or an auxiliary verb as in (b).

> (a) 서울에 계시는 선생님께 편지를 썼어요.
> (b) 아버지는 책을 읽고 계세요.

(2) 마음에 꼭 들다 literally means '(Someone/something) exactly enters the heart'. It is synonymous with the verb 좋아하다, though it never takes an object. Note that this is a verb, not an adjective, so its modifying form takes ~는, as in 마음에 드는 옷.

> 이런 신발이 마음에 꼭 들어요.
> 이런 신발을 좋아해요.

✎ Notes

· ·

· ·

· ·

· ·

· ·

· ·

CULTURE

한국의 의(衣)생활[1]   **The Korean life pertaining to clothes**

한국은 미국과 옷 문화[2]가 조금 다릅니다. 학교나 교회에 갈 때 그냥 슬리퍼[3]를 신거나 짧은 치마나 반바지, 또는 소매[4]가 없는 옷을 입는 것을 좋아하지 않습니다. 일을 하러 갈 때도 많은 사람들이 정장을 입습니다. 은행이나 우체국에서 일하는 사람들은 유니폼[5]을 입기도 합니다. 중고등학교에서는 보통 교복[6]을 입습니다. 어른[7]을 만날 때도 깨끗하고 단정한[8] 옷을 입으려고 합니다. 인터뷰할 때 남자는 넥타이를 매고[9] 정장을 입어야 하고, 여자도 단정한 치마 정장이나 바지 정장을 입고 화려하지[10] 않은 액세서리[11]를 합니다. 설날이나 결혼식 등의 특별한[12] 날에는 전통 옷인 한복을 입기도 합니다.

1. 의생활: clothing habits
2. 문화: culture
3. 슬리퍼: slipper
4. 소매: sleeve
5. 유니폼: uniform
6. 교복: school uniform

7. 어른: adult, (one's) elders
8. 단정하다: to be neat
9. 매다: to tie
10. 화려하다: to be fancy, colorful
11. 액세서리: accessory
12. 특별하다: to be special

USAGE

1   *Requesting, granting, and denying permission*

Requesting and granting permission

(1) 점원: 어서 오세요. 어떤 옷을 찾으세요?
성희: 구경 좀 해도 돼요?
점원: 그럼요. 구경하세요.
성희: 이 치마 한 번 입어 봐도 될까요?
점원: 네, 입어 보세요.

Asking permission

(2) A: 저어, 머리가 많이 아픈데 집에 일찍 가도 됩니까?
B: 많이 아파요? 그럼 집에 가서 쉬세요.

(3) A: 숙제를 내일까지 내도 돼요?
B: 내일까지 내면 안 돼요. 오늘 내세요.

(4) A: 여기 있는 신문 좀 봐도 될까요?
B: 네, 보세요.

Requesting and refusing

(5) A: 사전 있으면 좀 빌려 주실 수 있으세요?
B: 사전이 없는데요.

(6) A: 밖에 비가 많이 오는데, 우산 좀 빌려 주실래요?
B: 저도 지금 나가야 되기 때문에 . . . 죄송합니다.

You can also ask permission by ~(으)면 안 돼요/안 될까요?

A: 숙제를 아직 다 못 했는데 내일 내면 안 될까요?
B: 네, 좋아요. 내일 주세요.

A: 이 연습 문제가 어려운데 나중에 하면 안 돼요?
(연습 문제 'an exercise')
B: 안 돼요. 지금 하세요.

Here are different ways of making a request.

밖에 비가 오는데 우산이 없어요.

저어, 우산 있어요?

저어, 죄송하지만 우산 좀 . . .

혹시 우산 있으세요? (혹시 'by any chance')

우산 좀 빌려 주실래요?

우산 좀 빌려 주실 수 있으세요?

죄송하지만 우산 좀 빌려 주세요.

우산 좀 빌려도 될까요?

우산 좀 빌릴 수 있을까요?

우산 좀 빌렸으면 하는데요.

Exercise 1

Use any of the above expressions to ask your teacher to do the following:

(1)   lend you $20.00

(2)   accept a late homework assignment

(3)   speak Korean slowly

(4)   not make tests too difficult

(5)   write Korean characters clearly

(6)   lend you a Korean textbook

Exercise 2

Pair up and role-play for the following situations:

(1)   You just bought a black sweater at a department store. But you want to exchange it for a different color and style.

(2)   You are very hungry, but there is nothing to eat in the refrigerator except for the leftover Chinese food that your roommate brought from a Chinese restaurant last night. Ask your roommate for permission to eat it.

(3) You are taking a two-hour final exam for an intermediate Korean class. You need to go to the restroom in the middle of the exam. Ask your teacher for permission. (화장실 'restroom')

(4) You are at work and suddenly have a headache. You took a medicine, but it did not soothe. So you ask your boss for permission to leave early.

(5) You are a Korean businessman at a large corporation. You have an important meeting in twenty minutes, and there are a lot of things you want your secretary to do. But there are a couple of things she is not willing to do. Play the role of boss and secretary.

Exercise 3

Look at the following pictures and express prohibition.

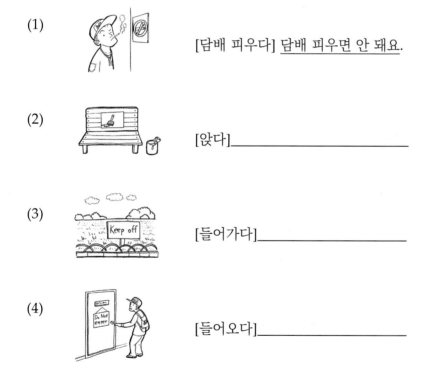

(1) [담배 피우다] 담배 피우면 안 돼요.

(2) [앉다]_____

(3) [들어가다]_____

(4) [들어오다]_____

Exercise 4

Express prohibition by ~지 마세요 or ~(으)면 안 돼요.
(열다 'to open', 끄다 'to turn off', 켜다 'to turn on', 버리다 'to throw away')

(1) _____

(2) _____

(3) _____

(4) _____

(5) _____

(6) _____

Notes

2   *Making plans*

(1) 성희: 민지 씨, 백화점에서 지금 세일을 하는데,
            같이 안 가 볼래요?

     민지: 마침 잘 됐네요. 바지를 하나 사려고 했는데 . . .
            성희씨는 뭐 살 거예요?

     성희: 투피스 한 벌하고 구두를 하나 살까 해요.

(2) A: 백화점에 언제 갈 거예요?

     B: 글쎄요, 내일 오후쯤 갈까 해요.

(3) A: 콘서트에 안 갈래요? 티켓(ticket)이 두 장 있어요.

     B: 고마워요. 같이 가요.

(4) A: 오늘 도서관에 갈 거예요?

     B: 네, 수업 끝나고 세 시쯤 가서 책 빌리려고 해요.

(5) A: 오늘 저녁은 나가서 먹어요?

     B: 네, 기숙사 친구들하고 한국 식당에 가기로 했어요.
            같이 갈래요?

(6) A: 선생님, 학기말 시험이 끝난 다음에 기숙사에서 파티 할
            건데 오실 수 있으세요?

     B: 네, 꼭 갈게요.

There are several ways of expressing one's intention.

할까 해요	I am thinking of doing . . .
하려고 해요	I plan to/intend to . . .
할 거예요	I will probably do . . .
할래요	I'll do . . .
할게요	I'd like to do . . . (volunteering)
하기로 했어요	I decided to do . . .

▶ **Exercise 1**

Role-play for the following situations.

> (1)   You want to go shopping at a 'Back to school' sale to buy
>   clothes, shoes, and stationery. Make a list of things to buy,
>   then call a friend to go shopping together.
> (2)   You and your friends are planning a surprise birthday
>   party for someone. There are a lot of things to prepare:
>   presents, cake, invitation cards, drinks, food, place,
>   etc. Organize the party.

▶ **Exercise 2**

Make plans, using the "intention" constructions.

> 지난 여름에는 여행을 할까 했는데, 시간도 없고 돈도 없어서 그냥 집에
> 있었어요. 이번 여름에는 꼭 뉴욕에 가려고 해요. 뉴욕에서 일하고 싶어서
> 뉴욕 월스트리트에 있는 회사(company)에 전화를 했어요. 다음 주에
> 인터뷰를 하기로 했어요.
>
> (1)   summer plan
> (2)   plan for next semester
> (3)   plan for a friend's birthday party
> (4)   plan for a weekend trip

Examples

3 | *Listening to weather forecasts*

> (1) A: 비가 오는 날 어떤 옷을 입으세요?
>   B: 청바지를 입고 긴 장화(boots)를 신어요.
>   A: 바람이 많이 부는 날은 어떤 옷을 입으세요?
>   B: 모자를 쓰고 스웨터를 입어요.
>
> (2) A: 결혼식(wedding)에 갈 때 어떤 옷을 입으세요?
>   B: 보통 정장을 입어요.

(3) A: 이 옷이 어때요?

   B: 잘 맞는데 소매(sleeve)가 길어요.

(4) A: 이 치마는 좀 긴 것 같아요.

   B: 아니에요. 요즘은 긴 치마가 유행이에요.

(5) A: 남자 친구가 어떻게 생겼어요?

   B: 키가 크고 잘 생겼어요. 영화 배우(actor) 같아요.

(6) A: 살이 빠진 것 같아요.

   B: 요즘 운동해요.

Useful expressions

뚱뚱하다	to be fat
날씬하다	to be thin
말랐다	to be skinny
살이 찌다	to gain weight
살이 빠지다	to lose weight
다이어트하다	to be on a diet
키가 크다	to be tall
키가 작다	to be short
예쁘다	to be pretty
잘생기다	to be handsome
멋있다	to be stylish
못생기다	to be ugly
소매가 길다	the sleeves are long
옷이 맞다	the clothes fit
치마가 길다	the skirt is long
치마가 짧다	the skirt is short

◗ **Exercise 1**

Interview your classmates.

(1) 부모님보다 키가 크세요?

(2) 동생 있어요? 어떻게 생겼어요? 나이는 몇이에요?

(3) 어느 남자/여자 배우(actor)가 제일 잘생겼어요/예뻐요?

(4) 어떤 사람과 결혼하고 싶어요?

(5) 키가 작은 농구 선구가 있습니까?

(6) 요즘 어떤 옷이 유행이에요?

(7) 못생긴 영화 배우가 있어요? 누구예요?

(8) 다이어트를 해 봤어요?

◗ **Exercise 2**

Converse with your classmates about their favorite outfits.

◗ **Exercise 3**

Choose several well-known people (e.g., celebrities, classmates, politicians, etc.). Let your classmates guess who you have in mind by giving them hints about their physical appearance.

◗ **Exercise 4**

Bring photos of your family or friends. Describe each person's physical appearance and outfits.

3 *Shopping*

(1) 옷 가게에서

A: 어서 오세요. 뭘 찾으세요?

B: 여름 티셔츠 좀 보려고요.

A: 이 쪽에 좋은 게 많이 있습니다.
무슨 색 찾으세요?

B: 노란색 있어요?

A: 노란색은 지금 없는데 다른 색으로 골라 보세요.

B: 그럼 하늘색으로 주세요. 얼마예요?

A: 정가(list price)는 이 만원인데 지금 세일이라서
만 오천원입니다.

(2) 구두 가게에서

A: 뭐 찾으세요?

B: 네. 일할 때 신을 편한 구두를 찾고 있는데요.

A: 무슨 사이즈(size) 신으세요?

B: 240으로 주세요.

Exercise 1

(Pair work) Engage in a dialogue between a store clerk and a customer to
shop for the following items.

(1) 긴 치마

(2) 운동복

(3) 목도리(muffler, scarf)와 장갑 (gloves)

(4) 정장 구두 (dress shoes)

(5) 와이셔츠와 넥타이 (dress shirt and necktie)

(6) 겨울 코트 (coat)

(7) 바지와 블라우스 (blouse)

Exercise 2

Ask your classmate the following questions and report the result to the class.

(1)   날씨가 추워지면 어떤 옷을 입으세요?

(2)   더운 여름에는 보통 어떤 옷을 입으세요?

(3)   봄 여름 가을 겨울 정장이 몇 벌이나 있어요?

(4)   신발이 모두 몇 켤레 있어요?

(5)   청바지가 모두 몇 벌 있어요?

(6)   신발 사이즈 뭐 신으세요?

(7)   옷을 얼마나 자주 사세요?

(8)   옷을 보통 어디에서 사세요?

(9)   갖고 있는 옷 중에서 비싼 옷이 어떤 옷이고 얼마예요?

(10) 갖고 있는 옷 중에서 가장 자주 입는 옷은 뭐예요?

Notes

Lesson 2 Clothing and Fashion

CONVERSATION 1 *I am going to buy clothes at the department store.*

Soobin makes a call to Minji.

Soobin:	Minji, there is a sale at the department store. Do you want to go together?
Minji:	Just in time; this worked out well. I was just preparing to go to the department store as well now. I am going to buy a suit. What are you going to buy?
Soobin:	I am going to buy a dress and a pair of dress shoes. I don't have clothes to wear these days.
Minji:	Neither do I. It is hard to choose clothes because Korea has a different style from Canada.
Soobin:	What kind of suit do you need, Minji?
Minji:	I have to buy a decent skirt suit because I have an interview.

CONVERSATION 2 *Miniskirts are trendy these days.*

Soobin and Minji are at the department store to buy clothes.

S.A.:	Welcome. What kind of clothes are you looking for?
Soobin:	Let me look around.
S.A.:	Okay, take your time to choose.
Soobin:	Well what kinds of skirts are trendy these days?
S.A.:	Miniskirts are trendy these days. How do you like this?
Soobin:	Do you have it in navy as well as in green?
S.A.:	Nowadays, bright colors are more popular than dark colors. How do you like the yellow or sky blue colors?
Soobin:	May I try both?
S.A.:	Yes, of course.
Soobin:	Minji, which color looks good on me?
Minji:	That sky blue color suits you better, Soobin.
Soobin:	Is that so? (To the sales assistant) Then, please give me the sky blue one.

* S.A. = Sales Assistant

NARRATION   *Shopping at the department store*

Today, Soobin went to the department store to buy clothes with her friend Minji. It was very crowded with people who came to shop at the department store. Soobin bought a miniskirt, which is trendy these days, a blouse, and high-heeled sandals; Minji bought a comfortable pair of pants to wear when she exercises, and T-shirts. It is hard to buy clothes because clothing trends change quickly in Korea. Minji bought a thin cotton jacket to give to her father, who is in Canada. The sale allowed her to buy it at half price. However, since she didn't have enough cash, she paid through her card. Soobin and Minji felt very good because they bought clothes that they liked at a cheap price.

CULTURE   *The Korean life pertaining to clothes*

Korea has a little different clothing culture from America. People don't like wearing slippers, miniskirts, short pants, or sleeveless clothes when going to school or church. Many people wear formal suits going to work. People who work at the banks or post offices tend to wear uniforms. Middle school and high school students usually wear school uniforms.

People try to wear clean and neat clothes when meeting elders. Men should wear a formal suit with a necktie, and women should wear a neat skirt suit or pantsuit without fancy accessories for an interview. People sometimes wear the traditional Korean costume, *hanbok*, on special days such as New Year's Day or a wedding ceremony.

3과 여행

Lesson 3 Travel

Conversation 1   한국에 가게 됐어요.

소피아는 뉴욕대학교 캠퍼스에서 마이클을 만났습니다.

Conversation 1

마이클:	안녕하세요, 소피아 씨.
소피아:	어, 마이클 씨.
	전화하려고 했는데 마침 잘 만났네요.
마이클:	무슨 일인데요?
소피아:	사실은 저 이번 여름에 한국에 가게 됐어요.G3.1
마이클:	그래요? 잘 됐네요. 참, 스티브도 서울에 있는데
	만나게 되면 스티브한테 제 안부 좀 전해 주세요.
소피아:	네, 그럴게요.
마이클:	비행기 표는 사셨어요?
소피아:	네, 벌써 예약했어요.
마이클:	한국까지 왕복에 얼마예요?
소피아:	1,600불이에요.
마이클:	비자는 필요 없어요?
소피아:	네, 여권만 있으면 돼요.G3.2

COMPREHENSION QUESTIONS

1. 소피아는 이번 여름에 어디에 갑니까?
2. 스티브는 지금 어디 있습니까?
3. 소피아는 비자를 받았습니까?

NEW WORDS

NOUN

국내선	domestic flight
국제선	international flight
무료	free
비자	visa
사실	fact, truth
손	hand
여권	passport
여행사	travel agency
예약(하다)	reservation
오랫동안	for a long time
왕복	round-trip
외국	foreign country
장학금	scholarship
짐	luggage, load
출발(하다)	departure
편도	one-way trip
표	ticket

VERB

다치다	to hurt
맞다	to be correct
싸다	② to pack, wrap
알아듣다	to understand, recognize
이해하다	to understand

ADJECTIVE

가볍다	to be light
무겁다	to be heavy

ADVERB

약	approximately
혼자	alone

SUFFIX

~(으)면 되다	all one needs is
~게 되다	turns out that

NEW EXPRESSIONS

1. 그럴게요 means 'I will do so', which is an abbreviated form of 그렇게 할게요.

2. 필요하다 'to need, be necessary' has two ways of negation such as 필요 없다 'to be unnecessary' and 안 필요하다 'to not need'. However, there is no expression 필요 있다.

Grammar

G3.1   ~게 되다: change or turn of events

(1) A: 요즘 뭐 하세요?   What are you doing these days?

　　B: 다음 달부터 학교   It turned out that I am going to
　　　　 도서관에서 일하**게**   work in the school library starting
　　　　 됐어요.   next month.

(2) A: 저 이번에 장학금을   I got offered a scholarship.
　　　　 받**게 됐어요**.   (*Lit.*, It turned out that I will
　　　　　　　　　　　　　　　 receive a scholarship.)

　　B: 그래요? 잘 됐네요.   Is that right? That's great.

(3) 외국어를 배우면 외국 문화를 더 잘 이해하**게 될 거예요**.

(4) A: 다음 달에 동생이랑 서울에 가는 거 맞지요?

　　B: 사실은 저 혼자 먼저 떠나**게 됐어요**.

Notes

1. 되다 literally means 'become' or 'turn out'. ~게 되다, literally meaning 'turn out to ~', 'come to ~', or 'get to ~', expresses a change in situation or turn of events. That is, a person was in one event and is now in another event. The change in situation or turn of events is mostly accidental or something that is independent of the person's will or volition. It is typically used in telling news.

2. ~게 되다 is mostly used with verbs.

3. ~게 되다 is compared with ~어지다 (G1.1), which combines mostly with adjectives and expresses a change of state.

날씨가 갑자기 추워졌어요.	It's become cold suddenly.
요즘은 일찍 어두워져요.	It gets dark earlier these days.
컴퓨터가 가벼워졌어요.	The computer got lighter.

Exercises

1. Indicate in Korean the changes in situation or turn of events that occurred in the given description.

(1) I was admitted to graduate school, and so I will be attending graduate school this fall semester.

이번 가을에 대학원에 가게 됐어요.

(2) I didn't like sports before, but now I like them.

_____

(3) If you leave now, you will arrive around 6 o'clock.

_____

(4) Michael cannot come because he is busy now, but later he will come.

_____

(5) I was going to study Korean here in America this summer. But it turned out that I get to go to Seoul to see Steve as well as to study Korean.

_____

2. State the changes of events that occurred as a result of the given events.

(1) [서울에서 부산까지 기차로 5시간 걸려요. 지금 4시예요.]

지금 출발하면 <u>부산에 9시에 도착하게 돼요/될 거예요</u>.

(2) A: 한국어를 얼마나 배우면 뉴스를 알아 듣게 돼요?

B: 약 2년만 배우면 _____
            (You will get to understand.)

(3) 손을 다쳤어요.

그래서 한 달동안 _____
            (I will not be able to play basketball.)

(4) 서울에 있는 한국어 여름 학교에서 장학금을 받았어요.

그래서 이번 여름에 _____

(5) 한국에 있는 친구들을 오랫동안 못 만났어요.

그런데, 이번에 한국에 가면 _____
            (I will get to see them.)

(6) 여행 가방이 너무 무거워요. 그래서 공항에서 돈을 더

_____.

G3.2 ~(으)면 되다 'have only to . . .', 'all one needs is . . .'

(1) A: 여행 준비 다 했어요?   Did you prepare everything
                                              for your trip?

    B: 네, 비자는 지난주에 받았고,   Yes, I got my visa last week,
        이젠 짐만 싸**면 돼요.**   and now I have only to pack
                                              my luggage.

(2) A: 한국 가는 비행기 표   How much is the air ticket to
        얼마예요?   Korea?

    B: 편도는 1,000불인데,   One way is $1,000, but all
        왕복은 1,200불만 내**면**   you need to pay for a round-
        돼요/ 주시**면 돼요.**   trip is $1,200.

(3) A: 여기 화장실이 어디예요?

    B: 저기 가운데 건물에서 왼쪽으로 가시**면 돼요.**

(4) 국내선은 3층, 국제선은 1층으로 가시**면 됩니다.**

✎ Notes

1. ~(으)면 되다, literally meaning 'It would do if . . .' or 'It would be all right/good if . . .', is used to tell what is needed to resolve a given situation.

2. N만 ~(으)면 되다 emphasizes the minimum that it takes to resolve the given situation. It is best translated as 'all I have to do is'.

Exercises

1. Complete the following sentences.

   (1) 한국어를 잘하고 싶으면 <u>한국 친구를 사귀면 돼요.</u>

   (2) 인터넷에서 무료로 책을 읽고 싶으면 _____

   (3) 길을 잘 모르면 _____

   (4) 전화번호를 모르면 _____

   (5) 도서관에서 음악을 들으려면 _____

   (6) 비행기 표를 예약하고 싶으면 여행사에 _____

2. Using ~(으)면 돼요 or N만 ~(으)면 돼요, complete the following dialogues, providing a resolution to the given situation.

   (1) A: 비행기 표 언제까지 사야 돼요?

        B: 예약은 하셨죠?

            <u>그럼 떠나기 2주 전까지만 사시면 돼요.</u>

   (2) A: 여행 준비 다 됐어요?

        B: 네, 이제 _____

   (3) A: 숙제할 게 많아요?

        B: 아니요, _____

   (4) A: 공항까지 직접 운전하실 거예요?

        B: 아니요, 시청에서 공항버스를 _____

   (5) A: 한국어를 잘하고 싶은데, 어떻게 하면 좋을까요?

        B: _____

Conversation 2   한국에 갔다 왔어요.

▌ 소피아가 여름 방학이 끝나고 다시 학교에 돌아왔습니다.

Conversation   2

유미: 소피아 씨, 방학 때 어디 갔었어요?[G3.3]

소피아: 네, 한국에 갔다 왔어요.

유미: 그랬어요? 좋았겠네요.

소피아: 네, 정말 볼 것도 많고 재미있었어요. 여행하는
          동안 맛있는 음식도 먹고 구경도 많이 했어요.

유미: 어디가 제일 좋았어요?

소피아: 여러 군데 다녔는데 제주도하고 경주가
          제일 기억에 남아요.

유미: 저도 어렸을 때 경주에 가 본 적이[G3.4] 있어요.
          그런데 제주도는 못 가 봤어요.

소피아: 그래요? 제주도도 정말 좋으니까[G3.5] 나중에
          꼭 한번 가 보세요.

COMPREHENSION QUESTIONS

1. 소피아는 방학 동안 무슨 일을 했습니까?
2. 소피아가 한국에서 여행한 곳 중에서 어디가 제일 기억에 남습니까?
3. 유미는 언제 경주에 가 보았습니까?

NEW WORDS

NOUN

걱정(하다)	worry, concern
경주	Gyeongju
경치	scenery, view
기억(하다)	memory
남	south
동	east
박물관	museum
북	north
서	west
섬	island
스트레스	stress
옛날	the old days
절	Buddhist temple
제주도	Jeju Island
호텔	hotel

INTERJECTION

와	wow

ADJECTIVE

기쁘다	to be joyful, glad
멋있다	to be stylish, cool
아름답다	to be beautiful
유명하다	to be famous
인상적이다	to be impressive

VERB

남다	to remain
다니다	② to get around
다녀오다	to go and get back
풀다	to relieve

ADVERB

아까	a while ago
주로	mostly, mainly
하나도	(not) at all

SUFFIX

~(으)니까	expresses reason
~어/아 본 적(이) 있다/없다	expresses past experience
~었었/았었/ㅆ었	remote past

NEW EXPRESSIONS

1. 군데 'place' is used as a counter for numeric expressions (한 군데, 열 군데, 여러 군데). Compare this with 장소 'place', which is an independent noun, and with 곳 or 데 'place', which has to be used with a modifying expression (이런 데, 저런 곳, 재미있는 데, 좋은 곳).

2. 갔다 오다 means 'to go and come back' as in:

학교에 갔다 왔어요.	I came back home from school.
작년에 한국에 갔다 왔어요.	I visited Korea last year.

Grammar

G3.3   Doubling of ~었-: ~었었-/~았었-/~ㅆ었-

Examples

(1) 민지: 방학 때 어디로 여행 **갔었**어요?
    마크: 제주도로 갔었어요.
    민지: 와, 재미있었겠네요!

(2) 제니: 마크 어디 갔어요?
    샌디: 커피 마시러 갔어요.
    (잠시 후에 마크가 돌아왔습니다)
    제니: 마크 씨, 어디 **갔었**어요?
    마크: 커피 마시러 **갔었**어요.

(3) 유미: 유진 씨, 스티브 씨 일어났어요?
    유진: 네, 일어났어요.
    유미: 마크 씨는요?
    유진: 아까 일어**났었**어요. 그런데 또 자요.

(4) 유미: 마크 씨 피아노 잘 쳐요?
    마크: 어렸을 때는 좀 **쳤었**는데 지금은 못 쳐요.

Notes

1. The doubling of ~었- (realized as ~었었-, ~았었- or ~ㅆ었-) is used in focusing on a past event whose effect is no longer relevant at the present moment. In (1), for example, Mark is now back, and the effect of his being gone is no longer felt. The use of single ~었- in this context could mean that Mark is still in 제주도. The same is true with (2).

2. Similarly in (3) and (4), ~었었- expresses a past situation that does not continue or is not true anymore. More examples are given below:

> 옛날에는 한국에 호랑이가 많았었어요. 지금은 호랑이가 없어요.
> 어렸을 때는 매일 공원에 놀러 갔었어요. 지금은 자주 못 가요.

Exercises

Complete the dialogues using ~었었-.

(1) 유미: 방학 때 뭐 했어요?

　　 샌디: [I went to Korea to study Korean.]

　　　　 <u>한국어 배우러 한국에 갔었어요</u>.

(2) A: 방학 때 뭐 했어요?

　　 B: _____

　　　　 [I went to Chicago to see a friend.]

(3) A: _____

　　　　 [Did you go to the party yesterday?]

　　 B: 아니요, 바빠서 못 갔어요.

(4) A: 요즘 야구장에 자주 가세요?

　　 B: _____

　　　　 [No. I used to go to the baseball stadium often but I haven't been able to go recently at all.]

(5) A: 민수는 그렇게 노래를 못 불러요?

　　 B: _____

　　　　 [He used to sing well . . . (I don't know why not now.)]

(6) A: 지금 밖에 날씨가 어때요?

　　 B: _____

　　　　 [It was windy a while ago, but now it is all right.]

(7) A: 보통 어떤 운동을 하세요?

　　 B: _____

　　　　 [I used to swim every day, but I just jog these days.]

G3.4   ~어/아 본 적(이) 있다/없다 'there has been an/no occasion of . . .'

(1)	A:	유럽에 <u>가 봤어요</u>?	Have you ever been to Europe?
	B:	네, 옛날에 **가 본 적이 있어요**. 박물관이 인상적이었어요.	Yes, I've been there in the past.
(2)	A:	제주도에 여행**가 본 적 있어요**?	Have you ever visited Jeju Island?
	B:	아니요, 못 <u>가 봤어요</u>.	No, I haven't.
	A:	제주도는 한국에서 가장 경치가 아름답고 유명한 섬이에요. 동서남북 어디에 가도 정말 멋있어요.	
(3)	A:	스티브 윌슨 아세요?	
	B:	이름은 들어 봤는데 아직 **만나 본 적은 없어요**.	His name sounds familiar, but I haven't met him yet.

Notes

1. Recall that ~어/아 보다 in the past tense (~어 봤어요) expresses a past experience, as underlined in (1) and (2). Also recall that ~(으)ㄴ 적이 있다 means '[As I recall] there has been an occasion of . . .' Together, ~어/아 본 적이 있다/없다 means 'There has been an/no occasion in which one has an/no experience of . . .' In questions, it is more appropriately translated as 'Have you ever . . . ?', as in (2).

2. The experience mentioned must be one retrieved out of long-term memory. It is usually accompanied by a time expression such as 작년에 'last year', 몇 달 전에 'a few months ago', or even 얼마 전에 'some time ago'. It would not be appropriate, however, to respond to the question 야구장에 가 본 적 있어요? with 지난 주에 가 본 적이 있어요, because it is too recent. It is not something to retrieve from long-term memory, but is in the speaker's current memory.

3. When the verb 보다 is used with ~어/아 본 적이 있다/없다 construction, V.S. ~어/아 part is omitted as in 본 적이 있다/없다. There is no such expression as 봐 본 적이 있다/없다.

Exercises

Answer the given questions using the ~어/아 본적이 있다/없다 structure.

(1) A: 절에 가 봤어요?

  B: <u>네, 한국에서 가 본 적이 있어요.</u>

(2) A: 오페라(opera) 들어 봤어요?

  B: _____

(3) A: 알래스카(Alaska)에 가 봤어요?

  B: _____

(4) A: 한복 입어 봤어요?

  B: _____

(5) A: 골프 쳐 봤어요?

  B: _____

(6) A: 스키 타 봤어요?

  B: _____

G3.5 ~(으)니까: expressing a reason or logical sequence

[Expressing reason]

(1) A: 비가 많이 오**니까** Because it's raining a lot,
        운전할 때 조심하세요. please drive carefully.

  B: 네, 걱정하지 마세요.

(2) A: 호텔에 같이 점심 먹으러 갈래요?

  B: 저는 좀 전에 먹었으**니까** 수지 씨랑 같이 가세요.

(3) 시간이 없으**니까** Since we don't have much
    택시를 타고 갈까요? time, shall we go by taxi?

[Temporal sequence]

(4) 소연: 주로 무슨 운동을 해요?
    성희: 요즘은 수영 배우고 있어요.
    해 보**니까** 스트레스를 When I tried swimming,
    풀 수 있어서 좋아요. I found that it relieves stress.

(5) A: 어제 일찍 잤어요?

  B: 아니요, 어제 집에 들어가**니까** 벌써 밤 12시였어요.

Notes

1. In examples (1) – (3), ~(으)니까 specifies a reason or ground for why the subsequent message is said. By appealing to a reason that is obvious or familiar to the listener, the speaker justifies and strengthens the validity of what is said subsequently. ~(으)니까 is conveniently translated as 'since', 'now that', 'given that', and 'because'.

2. It is frequently used in giving an excuse, explanation, or justification for a command or request to make your command sound more convincing and persuasive as in examples (1) – (3).

3. In examples (4) and (5), ~(으)니까 expresses a temporal sequence; that is, one situation temporally follows another. With A~(으)니까 B, the speaker's viewpoint is at the time of the occurrence of event A so that the speaker witnesses the occurrence of event B, as if the speaker is going through these events. That is to say, the two events are not just sequentially connected, but connected through the speaker's experience because event A leads the speaker to witness or experience event B.

4. It should be noted that ~(으)니까 in (4) and (5) is not marked for time even when it refers to a past event. This is because the speaker is describing the two sequential events as if he/she is currently witnessing them as he/she is going through these events.

Notes

· ·

· ·

· ·

· ·

· ·

· ·

Exercises

1. Using the ~(으)니까 form, complete the discourse.

(1) A: 뭐 타고 갈까요?

B: <u>지금 시간에는 길이 막히니까</u> 지하철을 타요.

(2) A: 저, 시간 있으면 오늘 좀 만날 수 있을까요?

B: _____ 내일 만나면 안 될까요?

A: 네, 그럼 내일 봐요.

(3) A: 이 선생님 계세요?

B: _____ 이따가 오후에 오세요.

(4) A: 거기까지 가는 버스 있어요?

B: 직접 가는 _____ 지하철을 타세요.

(5) A: 한국에 언제 가세요?

B: _____ 일주일 후에 가요.

(6) A: 저한테서 빌린 비디오 언제 돌려 주실 거예요?

B: _____ 다음 주에 돌려 드릴게요.

2. Using ~(으)니까, provide an event that leads to witnessing the given situation.

(1) A: 언니한테 전화했어요?

B: 네. <u>오랜만에 전화하니까</u> 언니가 너무 기뻐했어요.

(2) 소연: 민지 씨, 어디 아파요?

민지: 아니요, 시험 때문에 매일 늦게까지 책을
_____ 좀 피곤해요.

(3) 성희: 소연 씨, 요즘 굉장히 좋아 보여요.

소연: 네. 요즘 매일 수영해요.
_____ 스트레스도 풀 수 있고 몸이 가벼워져서 참 좋아요.

(4) A: 성희 씨 만났어요? 아까 도서관에서 찾던데요.

B: 아니요, 못 만났어요. _____ 벌써 가고 없었어요.

Narration | 소피아의 한국 여행

저는 한국에 있는 동안 경주와 제주도에 다녀왔습니다.
경주는 옛날 신라[1]의 수도[2]입니다. 한국에는 절이 많이
있는데, 경주의 불국사[3]가 가장 유명하고 아름답습니다.
특히 소피아는 불국사에 있는 다보탑[4]과 석가탑[5]이
인상적이었습니다. 제주도는 한국에서 가장 큰 섬입니다.
서울에서 비행기로 한 시간 정도 걸립니다. 제주도는 남쪽에
있어서 날씨가 따뜻하고 경치가 아름답습니다. 저는 여러
곳을 구경했는데, 그 중에서 섬 가운데에 있는 한라산[6]이 가장
마음에 들었습니다. 참 즐거운 여행이었습니다.

1. 신라: Silla Kingdom
2. 수도: capital city
3. 불국사: Bulguksa
4. 다보탑: Dabo Tower
5. 석가탑: Seokga Tower
6. 한라산: Halla Mount

COMPREHENSION QUESTIONS

1. 소피아는 한국에서 어디로 여행을 갔습니까?
2. 불국사는 어떤 곳입니까?
3. 어느 곳이 가장 인상적이었습니까?
4. 서울에서 제주도까지 얼마나 걸립니까?
5. 제주도는 어떤 곳입니까?

NEW EXPRESSIONS

인상적 'impressive' consists of 인상 'impression' and the suffix ~적. Some Sino-Korean nouns take the suffix ~적, whose meaning is similar to "~ive" or "~ic" in English, and have the following pattern.

Adjective		Modifier	Adverb
인상적이다	to be impressive	인상적인	인상적으로
적극적이다	to be positive	적극적인	적극적으로
소극적이다	to be passive	소극적인	소극적으로

Notes

. . . .

. . . .

. . . .

. . . .

. . . .

. . . .

CULTURE

경주   The ancient capital of the Silla Kingdom

경주는 역사가 아주 오래된 도시입니다. 경주는 기원전(B.C.) 57년부터 서기
(A.D.) 935년까지 신라의 수도[1] 였습니다. 신라는 오래 전에 한반도(Korean
Peninsula)에 있던 세 나라 중 하나입니다. 신라는 과학[2], 문화, 예술[3] 이
발달[4] 하였습니다. 경주에는 신라 시대[5] 의 불교[6] 문화 예술과 건축물[7] 들이
지금까지도 많이 남아있습니다[8].

UNESCO (United Nations Educational, Scientific, and Cultural
Organization)는 2000년에 '경주 역사 유적 지구(Gyeongju Historic Areas)'
를 '세계 유산(World Heritage Site)'으로 지정하였습니다[9]. 특히[10] 불국사와
석굴암[11] 은 신라 시대의 아름답던 불교 문화를 보여 주는 건축물로 아주
유명합니다. 경주에는 별[12] 과 하늘을 볼 수 있는 아시아[13] 에서 가장 오래된
건축물인 첨성대도 있습니다. 경주는 도시가 하나의 박물관 같습니다.

1. 수도: capital city   2. 과학: science
3. 예술: art   4. 발달(하다): development
5. 시대: period   6. 불교: Buddhism
7. 건축물: building, structure   8. 남아 있다: to be neat
9. 지정하다: to appoint   10. 특히: particularly
11. 석굴: stone cave   12. 별: star
13 아시아: Asia

USAGE

1 *Calling a travel agency and buying an airline ticket*

Example

(샌디가 비행기 표를 예약하려고 여행사에 전화합니다.)

직원:　　여행사입니다.
샌디:　　여보세요.
　　　　　저, 서울 가는 비행기표 좀 예약하고 싶은데요.
직원:　　몇 분이 가십니까?
샌디:　　한 사람인데요.
직원:　　언제 떠나십니까?
샌디:　　6월 2일에 출발해서 7월 31일에 돌아오려고 하는데요.
　　　　　왕복에 얼마예요?
직원:　　1350불입니다. 예약해 드릴까요?
샌디:　　네. 예약해 주세요.
직원:　　성함하고 카드 번호 좀 불러 주시겠어요?
샌디:　　네. (잠시 후)
직원:　　출발 1주일 전에 오셔서 티켓 찾아가시면 됩니다.
샌디:　　고맙습니다.

(1) Making a reservation

_____(Destination) 가는 비행기표 예약하려는데요/예약했으면 하는데요.

(2) Giving departure and return dates

____ 월 _____일에 출발해서 _____월 _____일에 돌아오려고 하는데요.
(Departure date)　　　　　　(Return date)

(3) Asking about airfare

_____ (airline)은/는 얼마예요?

대한항공은 얼마예요	How much is Korean Airline (KAL)?
(항공료가) 얼마예요?	How much is the airfare?
값은 어떻게 돼요?	What's the fare?

(4) Choosing an airline

A: 어느 항공편 이용하시겠습니까?

어느 비행기요? or 어느 비행기로 가시겠습니까?

Which airline would you like to use?

B: _____(name of an airline)(으)로 해 주세요.

Useful words

편도 one way, 항공료 airfare, 출발 departure, 도착 arrival, 항공편 an airline, 좌석 a seat, 창가 좌석 a window seat, 항공권/티켓/비행기표 an airline ticket, 일등석 a first class (seat), 일반석 an economy class (seat)

Exercise 1

(Role-play) Make a dialogue between a customer and a travel agent for the following situations:

(1) Customer wants to reserve two round-trip plane tickets from Seoul to Chicago.

(2) Customer wants to buy a one-way plane ticket from New York to Seoul.

2 *Talking about vacation and summer jobs*

샌디 : 영미 씨, 오래간만이에요.

여름 방학 잘 보냈어요?

영미: 백화점에서 아르바이트 (part-time job) 했어요.

샌디: 무슨 아르바이트 했어요?

영미: 백화점에서 일했어요.

샌디씨는 방학 때 어디 다녀 왔어요?

샌디: 한국에 갔다 왔어요.

영미: 그랬어요? 재미있었어요?

샌디: 네, 근데 날씨 때문에 좀 고생했어요.

영미: 왜요? 날씨가 어땠는데요?

샌디: 한국 여름 날씨가 너무 더웠어요.

 **Exercise 1**

Converse with your partner regarding the past summer vacation.

Exercise 2

Exchange the following information with your classmates. Write down the answers and report them to the class.

    (1)   여름 방학 동안 아르바이트 해 본 적 있으세요?

    (2)   왜 아르바이트 했어요?

    (3)   어디서 일했어요?

    (4)   무슨 일을 했어요?

    (5)   일주일에 몇 시간 일했어요?

    (6)   얼마나 벌었어요?

    (7)   앞으로 어떤 아르바이트를 하고 싶으세요?

Exercise 3

가장 기억에 남는 여행에 대해서 (about) 얘기해 보세요.

Notes

. . . .

. . . .

. . . .

. . . .

. . . .

. . . .

3   *Describing past events*

(1) A: 여름 방학 때 어디 갔다 왔어요?

B: 한국에 갔다 왔어요.

A: 그랬어요? 한국에 얼마 동안 있었어요?

B: 두 달 있었어요.

A: 한국에 있는 동안 여행 많이 했어요?

B: 네, 여러 군데 다녔어요.

A: 재미있었겠네요. 어디가 제일 좋았어요?

B: 경주가 제일 인상적이었어요.

(2) 지난 여름 방학 동안 한국에 갔다 왔어요. 6월 말에 가서 8월 30일에
미국에 돌아왔어요. 한국에 가 본 적이 없었기 때문에 처음에는
약간 걱정이 됐어요. 서울에서 두 달 동안 한국어를 배웠는데 참
재미있었어요. 한국에 있는 동안 친구들도 많이 사귀었어요.
친구들하고 여행도 많이 했어요. 부산에도 가고 경주에도
놀러 갔어요. 내년 여름에도 한국에 가고 싶어요.
(걱정이 됐어요 was worried)

Exercise 1

Take the roles of 영미 and 샌디.

영미: _____?

샌디: 서울에 갔다 왔어요.

영미: _____?

샌디: 한국어 배우러 갔어요.

영미: _____?

샌디: 여러 군데 갔어요.

영미: _____?

샌디: 경주가 제일 좋았어요.

영미: _____?

샌디: 지난 주말에 돌아왔어요.

Exercise 2

Pair up and look at your schedule book for the past summer. Ask each other questions about your activities during the past summer.

Exercise 3

Converse with your partner about your and his/her past experiences in the following areas.

(1) 외국 여행 경험
(2) 아르바이트 경험 (experience)
(3) 가장 기억에 남는 생일 파티/선물
(4) 가장 인상적인 선생님

Exercise 4

Write a letter to your Korean teacher about your most recent summer vacation and read it to the class.

4 *Skimming newspaper ads for airline tickets and travel information*

(Sandy is looking for a round-trip airline ticket from New York to Seoul and is reading the following ads in a Korean newspaper.)

> 뉴서울 여행사
>
> 뉴욕-서울행 항공권 특별 세일 $799
> 미국-한국 왕복 가장 싼 가격
> 미국 국내선 가장 싼 가격
> 유럽, 남미, 동남아 전세계 비행기표
> 서울 출발 미국행 비행기표
> 서울, 동남아, 미국 내 호텔 예약 할인
> 전화 (800) 790-4236
>
> 티켓 무료 배달해 드립니다.

(국내선 domestic airline, 남미 South America, 동남아 Southeast Asia, 할인 a discount, 무료 배달 free delivery)

▶ Exercise 1

Make a telephone conversation with a travel agent (your partner) based on the ad.

▶ Exercise 2

Read the ad above and mark the following statements as T(rue) or F(alse).

(1) The 뉴서울 travel agency offers a special sale price for round-trip tickets from New York to Seoul. _____

(2) The travel agency also arranges hotel reservations. _____

(3) There will be a charge for ticket delivery. _____

(4) The travel agency offers a special sale price for tickets from Seoul to the United States. _____

✎ Notes

. . . .

. . . .

. . . .

. . . .

. . . .

. . . .

Lesson 3 Travel

CONVERSATION 1 *It turned out that I am going to Korea.*

Sophia met Michael at the campus of New York University.

Michael: How are you, Sophia. Where are you going?
Sophia: Oh, Michael, I was going to call you. I met you just in time.
Michael: Why?
Sophia: In fact, it turned out that I'm going to Korea this summer.
Michael: Is that so? Good for you. By the way, Steve is in Seoul. If you meet him, please say hi to him.
Sophia: Yes, I will.
Michael: Did you buy the flight ticket?
Sophia: Yes, I already made a reservation.
Michael: How much is the round-trip to Korea?
Sophia: It's 1,600 dollars.
Michael: You don't need a visa?
Sophia: No. Just a passport will be okay.

CONVERSATION 2 *I have been to Korea.*

Sophia returned to school after summer vacation.

Yumi: Sophia, have you been anywhere during the vacation?
Sophia: Yes, I have been to Korea.
Yumi: Was that so? It must have been nice.
Sophia: Yes, there were so many things to see and it was fun. While I was traveling I ate delicious foods, and I went sightseeing a lot.
Yumi: Which place did you like most?
Sophia: I went to many places. Jeju Island and Gyeongju are the most memorable.
Yumi: I have been to Gyeongju when I was young, but I have never been to Jeju Island.
Sophia: Is that so? Definitely visit Jeju Island because it is also great.

NARRATION   *Sophia's trip to Korea*

I have been to Gyeongju and to Jeju Island during my stay in Korea. Gyeongju is the capital city of old Silla. There are many temples in Korea, but Bulguksa in Gyeongju is the most famous and beautiful. Dabo Tower and Seokga Tower at Bulguksa were especially impressive to me.

Jeju Island is the biggest island in Korea. It takes about one hour from Seoul to get there by airplane. Since Jeju Island is on the southern end, the weather is warm. Also, the scenery is beautiful. I went sightseeing at several places. Among them, I liked Halla Mount in the middle of the island. It was a very pleasant trip.

CULTURE   경주

Gyeongju is a city with a very long history. Gyeongju was the capital city of Silla from 57 B.C. to A.D 935. Silla is one of the three kingdoms that existed on the Korean Peninsula a long time ago. Silla had advanced science, culture, and art. Many artifacts of Buddhist culture and architecture of Silla can still be seen in Gyeongju.

UNESCO (United Nations Educational, Scientific, and Cultural Organization) designated the Gyeongju Historic Areas as a World Heritage Site in 2000. Bulguksa and Seokguram have very famous architecture that shows the beautiful Buddhist culture of Silla. There is the oldest architecture in Asia, from which you can see the stars and the sky. Gyeongju is a city that is like a museum.

4과 한국 생활 I

Lesson 4 Life in Korea I

Conversation 1   인사동에 가는 길이에요.

▍민지는 기숙사 입구에서 우진이를 우연히 만났습니다.

Conversation   1

민지: 우진 씨, 어디 가세요?

우진: 선물 사러 인사동에 가는 길이에요.G4.1

민지: 누구 선물이에요?

우진: 이 달 말이 엄마 생신이거든요.G4.2

민지: 아, 그래요? 뭘 사실 건데요?

우진: 수저 세트 어떨까요?

민지: 그거 좋은 생각이네요. 인사동에 가면 한국
         전통 공예품 가게들이 많으니까 마음에 드는
         걸 살 수 있을 거예요.

우진: 혹시 지금 시간이 되면 저하고 같이 가실래요?

민지: 네, 같이 가요. 그런데 제가 가는 길에
         은행에서 돈을 좀 찾아야 되는데 괜찮으시겠어요?

우진: 네, 그럼요.

COMPREHENSION QUESTIONS

1. 우진이는 왜 선물을 사려고 합니까?
2. 우진이는 무엇을 사고 싶어합니까?
3. 우진이와 민지는 왜 인사동에서 선물을 사려고 합니까?
4. 민지는 가는 길에 무엇을 하려고 합니까?

NEW WORDS

NOUN

계좌	account
공예품	handicraft item
몸	body
병원	hospital
성적	grade
세트	a set
소포	parcel
수저	spoon and chopsticks
숟가락	spoon
신분증	identification card
유학생	student abroad
인사동	Insadong
전통	tradition
젓가락	chopsticks
직원	staff, employee
하루 종일	all day
학비	tuition

VERB

바빠지다	to get busier
생기다	to be formed
잊다	to forget
졸리다	to feel sleepy
(돈을) 찾다	to withdraw money
익숙하다	to be familiar

ADJECTIVE

편안하다	to be comfortable

ADVERB

우연히	by chance
항상	always
혹시	by any chance

SUFFIX

~거든요	you see (because)
~는 길이다	(be) on one's way

NEW EXPRESSIONS

1. 수저 is a combination of 숟가락 'spoon' and 젓가락 'a pair of chopsticks'.

2. 시간이 되다 'to have enough time, to be available' as in 이번 주말에 시간이 되세요? 'Are you available this weekend?'

3. 돈을 찾다 means 'to withdraw money' from a bank account. 돈을 빼다 'to remove, take out' is used instead if you withdraw cash from an ATM.

Grammar

G4.1   ~는 길이다/~는 길에 '(be) on one's way'

(1) A: 어디 가세요?   Where are you going?

     B: 소포 부치러   우체국에 I'm on my way to the post office

           가**는 길이에요.**   to mail this package.

(2) A: 어디 가세요?

     B: 몸이 아파서 병원에 가**는 길이에요.**

(3) A: 오늘 은행에 갈 거예요?

     B: 네, 이따가 오후에 갈 건데요.

     A: 그럼 은행 갔다 오**는 길에** 주스 좀 사 올래요?

     B: 그럴게요.

Notes

1. 길 literally means 'a way, a road, a street'. Combined with a movement verb like 가다, 오다, 갔다 오다, ~는 길에 means 'on one's way (back from/to)'. ~는 길이에요 means '. . . is on one's way'.

> . . . 에 가는/오는 길에   on one's way to/back to . . .
>
> . . . 에서 오는 길에   on one's way back from . . .

2. In the original usage of ~는 길에/~는 길이에요, one is in the middle of going or coming to/from a location, as in (1) and (2). The expression, however, can also be used to mean 'since one is going to . . .', as in (3).

Exercises

1. Two people run into each other. Using ~는 길이에요, answer each question with the given location.

    (1) A: 어디 가세요?

           B: [school] <u>학교 가는 길이에요.</u>

    (2) A: 어디 가세요?

           B: [library] _____

    (3) A: 어디 갔다 오세요?

           B: [a store] _____

    (4) (학교에서 수업이 다 끝났습니다.)

           A: 집에 가세요?

           B: [home] 네, _____

    (5) A: 지금 학교에서 오세요?

           B: 아니요, [a friend's house] _____

2. You would like to ask your friend to do something for you on his/her way (back) from/to some place. Make up your request based on the given information.

    (1) 민지: 우진 씨, 우체국 안 가요?

           우진: 아, 잊어 버렸어요. 오후에 가야겠네요.

           민지: <u>그럼, 우체국 가는 길에 빵 좀 사 줄래요?</u> [빵]

           우진: 그럴게요.

    (2) A: 어디 가세요?

           B: 집 앞에 있는 가게에 가요.

           A: 그럼, _____ [편지/부치다]

    (3) A: 어디 가세요?

           B: 책 빌리러 도서관에 가요.

           A: 그럼, _____ [물/사다]

    (4) A: 어디 가세요?

           B: 소포 부치러 우체국에 가는 길이에요.

           A: 그럼, _____ [책/빌려 오다]

G4.2   ~거든요 'you see, (because)~'

(1) A: 요즘 많이 바빠졌네요.

   B: 네, 주말에는 하루 종일 일해요.

   A: 왜요?

   B: 학비가 많이 올랐**거든요**.

(2) 학생: 은행 계좌 만들고 싶은데요.

   직원: 신분증 좀 주시겠어요?

   학생: 제가 유학생이**거든요**. 여권도 괜찮을까요?

   직원: 그럼요.

(3) (at a restaurant table)

   A: 여기 두 명 더 오**거든요**.

         숟가락, 젓가락 좀 더 갖다 주시겠어요?

   B: 네. 금방 갖다 드릴게요.

(4) A: 한국 생활이 어떠세요?

   B: 많이 편안해졌어요.

         이제는 한국 문화에 익숙하**거든요**.

Notes

1. The ~거든요 sentence often provides a reason or explanation why the situation currently at issue is the way it is.

2. The reason or explanation provided must be something that the listener would understand easily when he/she hears it. ~거든요 is used when the speaker expects the listener to easily recognize the correlation between the situation currently at issue and the reason/explanation provided. It is roughly equivalent to saying in English 'You see, (because) . . .'

Exercises

1. Make up a response that explains the situation currently at issue.

(1) A: 왜 기분이 안 좋으세요?

B: <u>시험을 잘 못 봤거든요.</u>

(2) A: 봄 방학 때 집에 안 가세요?

B: 못 가요. _____

(3) A: 왜 한국어를 배우세요?

B: _____

(4) A: 무슨 비행기로 가세요?

B: 항상 대한항공(Korean Air)으로 가요.

_____

(5) A: (수영장에서) 왜 수영 안 하세요?

B: _____

(6) A: 저 이번에 장학금을 받게 됐어요.

B: 그래요? 어떻게 받았어요?

A: 성적이 _____

2. Make up a question that is appropriate for the given context.

(1) A: <u>많이 졸리세요?</u>

B: 네, 어제 잠을 세 시간밖에 못 잤거든요.

(2) A: _____?

B: 한국 친구가 생겼거든요.

(3) A: _____?

B: 얼굴이 예쁘거든요.

(4) A: _____?

B: 저하고 별로 안 친하거든요.

(5) A: _____?

B: 오늘 저녁에 파티가 있거든요.

Conversation 2   소포를 부치려고 하는데요.

▶ 우진이가 미국에 소포를 부치려고 우체국에 갔습니다.

Conversation   2

직원: 어서 오세요. 어떻게 도와 드릴까요?

우진: 미국으로 소포를 부치려고 하는데
          얼마나 걸릴까요?

직원: 미국 어디요?G4.3

우진: 뉴욕이요.

직원: 사흘 정도 걸려요.

우진: 그래요? 그 정도면 괜찮네요.

직원: 소포 안에 뭐가 들었어요? 깨지기 쉬운 거예요?

우진: 아니에요. 수저 세트예요.

직원: (종이를 주면서) 소포 보내시려면G4.4
          여기에 주소 좀 적어 주세요.

우진: 네, 여기 있습니다. 수고하세요.
          (우진이가 떠납니다.)

직원: 고객님, 잠깐만요. 영수증 가져가셔야지요.G4.5

우진: 아, 네. 감사합니다.

COMPREHENSION QUESTIONS

1. 우진이는 왜 우체국에 갔습니까?
2. 소포는 뉴욕까지 얼마나 걸립니까?
3. 우진이는 소포로 무엇을 부쳤습니까?

NEW WORDS

NOUN

고객	customer
등기	registered mail
보통	② regular
사흘	three days
상자	box
영수증	receipt
우체통	postbox
우편	mail
적응(하다)	to adapt
정도	approximate
졸업식	commencement
종이	paper
주소	address
핸드폰	cellular phone

VERB

가져가다	to take, carry
깨지다	to break
도와 드리다 *hon.*	to help
들어 있다	to contain
사용하다	to use
서다	to stand
적다	② to write down

ADJECTIVE

똑같다	to be identical
비슷하다	to be similar
정확하다	to be accurate
친하다	to be close (to)
특별하다	to be special

SUFFIX

(이)요	It is [noun].
~(으)려면	if . . . intends to
~어/아야지요	expresses obligation

NEW EXPRESSIONS

1. 부치다 to mail   (편지를 부쳐요.)
   붙이다 to stick, affix   (소포에 우표를 붙여요.)

2. 하루 one day   이틀 two days
   사흘 three days   나흘 four days

Grammar

G4.3   N(이)요 'It is [noun]'.

(1) [우체국에서]

직원: 상자 안에 <u>뭐</u>가 들어있어요?   What's in the box?

우진: <u>옷</u>**이요**. (옷 들어있어요./옷이에요.)   Clothes.

(2) A: <u>어디</u>까지 가세요?   How far are you
                                                   going?

B: <u>서울역</u>**이요**. (서울역까지 가요.)   To Seoul Station.

(3) A: <u>몇 학년</u>이에요?   What year are you in?

B: <u>일학년</u>**이요**. (일학년이에요.)   Freshman/first year.

(4) A: <u>전공</u>이 뭐예요?   What is your major?

B: <u>한국 역사</u>**요**. (한국 역사예요.)   Korean history.

Notes

1. N(이)요 is used to give the simplest answer to a question by mentioning only the very item in question (underlined) without having to repeat whatever else is mentioned in the question. Compare this with the full answer provided in parentheses.

2. N이요 is used after a consonant, as in (1) – (3) and N요 after a vowel, as in (4). Speakers of some dialects may use 요 in both cases.

Exercises

Give the simplest answer to the given question.

(1) A: 무슨 운동을 좋아해요?

    B: <u>야구요</u>.

(2) A: 이거 누가 만들었어요?

    B: _____.

(3) A: 이번 학기에 한국어 누가 가르치세요?

    B: _____.

(4) A: 이거 등기로 하실래요, 보통으로 하실래요?

    B: _____.

(5) A: 어제 저녁에 뭐 먹었어요?

    B: _____.

(6) A: 어느 식당을 제일 좋아해요?

    B: _____.

G4.4　~(으)려면 'if . . . intends to do'

(1) (우체국에서)

    손님:　우편으로 책을 보내**려면** 어떻게 해야 돼요?

    직원:　여기에 받는 사람 이름과 정확한 주소를 써 주세요.

(2) A: 한국 전통 공예품을 사**려면** 어디가 좋아요?

    B: 인사동에 가 보세요. 공예품을 많이 팔아요.

(3) A: 이거랑 똑같은 가방 있으세요?

    B: 똑같은 걸 사시**려면** 백화점에 가셔야 돼요

    A: 그러면 그냥 비슷한 걸로 주세요.

(4) 수업에 늦지 않**으려면** 밤에 일찍 자야 돼요.

Examples

Exercises

1. Complete the following sentences.

    (1) 소포를 부치려면 <u>우체국에 가야 돼요</u>.

    (2) 한국어를 잘하려면 _____

    (3) 건강해지려면 _____

    (4) 새 핸드폰을 사려면 _____

    (5) 친구한테 특별한 선물을 하려면 _____

    (6) 약속 시간에 늦지 않으려면 _____

    (7) 물건을 싸게 사려면 _____

    (8) 외국어를 배우려면 _____

2. Complete the following sentences using ~(으)려면.

    (1) <u>학교에 9시까지 가려면</u> 집에서 8시에 떠나야 돼요.

    (2) _____ 음식을 잘 먹어야 돼요.

    (3) _____ 한국에 가야 돼요.

    (4) _____ 우체국에 가야 돼요.

    (5) _____ 지하철을 타야 돼요.

    (6) _____ 우체통에 넣어야 돼요.

G4.5   ~어야/아야지요 'definitely/indeed/ought to/have to'

Examples

    (1) A: 서 있지 말고 여기 앉아서 기다리세요.

        B: 아니요, 괜찮아요. 이제 그만 가**야지요**.

    (2) A: 오늘 밤 늦게까지 공부할 거예요?

        B: 아니요, 피곤한데 자**야지요**.

    (3) (Someone is helping you repair your computer. Since it is getting quite late, you know he/she must go, although you hope he/she would stay a bit longer.)

        You: 늦었는데 가 보셔**야지요**?

        Guest: 괜찮아요. 좀 더 있어도 돼요.

    (4) A: 한국에서 살기가 쉽지 않네요.

        B: 한국 생활에 빨리 적응하려면 친구를 많이 사귀**어야지요**.

✦ Notes

1. ~어야/아야 refers to a person's obligation to do something or the necessity of a situation. ~지요 indicates the speaker's subjective judgment in the sense of 'indeed/certainly/ definitely/surely so', or 'of course'. Put together as ~어야/아야지요, the speaker shows his/her subjective judgment that the situation in question ought to happen.

2. It is often used in giving advice or a strong suggestion, as in (4).

Exercise

Complete the following dialogues using the ~어야/아야지요 form.

(1) (In a crowded restaurant)

　　A:　자리가 없네요.

　　B:　예약 안 하셨어요? 주말에는 <u>예약을 하셔야지요</u>.

(2) (A guest at your place is about to leave. It is a Korean social norm to ask the guest to stay longer.)

　　Host:　왜 벌써 가시려고 하세요?

　　Guest: 너무 늦었는데 이제 그만 _____

(3) A:　파티에 안 가세요?

　　B:　내일 시험이 있는데 _____

(4) A:　민수 졸업식에 안 가세요?

　　B:　나하고 제일 친한 친구인데 _____

(5) A:　밤 공기가 너무 차네요.

　　B:　문을 _____.

Narration 우진이의 편지

보고 싶은 엄마,

그동안 안녕하셨어요? 저는 몸 건강히 잘 지내고 있어요.
먼저 엄마 생신 축하 드려요. 한국에서 예쁜 수저 세트를
샀어요. 엄마 마음에 드셨으면 좋겠어요.

지난 번에 전화하셨을 때 제가 전화를 안 받아서 걱정 많이
하셨지요? 그 때 도서관에서 하루 종일 공부하고 있었어요.
이번 학기에 성적이 잘 나와서 장학금을 받게 됐어요. 학비는
안 보내 주셔도 돼요. 학교 생활에도 많이 적응했고 친구들도
많이 생겼어요. 그러니까 제 걱정은 하지 마세요. 그리고
항상 건강하세요. 가족들 모두 보고 싶어요.

그럼 또 연락 드릴게요. 안녕히 계세요.

2020년 6월 30일

서울에서
우진 올림

COMPREHENSION QUESTIONS

1. 이 편지는 누가 누구에게 보내는 것입니까?
2. 우진이는 어머니 생신에 무슨 선물을 드렸습니까?
3. 우진이는 어머니가 전화했을 때 어디에 있었습니까?
4. 우진이는 왜 학비를 안 받아도 됩니까?

Notes

· ·

· ·

· ·

· ·

· ·

CULTURE

인사동

한국의 전통 문화[1]와 음식을 맛보려면[2] 인사동에 꼭 가 봐야 합니다. 인사동은 서울 안국역에서 종로 2가까지 이르는[3] 거리[4]인데 한국의 전통 공예품[5]과 골동품[6] 가게들이 많은 곳입니다. 지하철 3호선을 타고 안국역에서 내려서 인사동으로 걸어가면 됩니다.

인사동에는 골동품과 공예품 가게들도 많지만 화랑[7], 전통 찻집[8], 전통 음식점들도 많습니다. 인사동 거리를 걸으면 공예품을 구경하는 학생들, 물건들을 고르는 외국인들, 전통 찻집에서 데이트를 하는 대학생들, 그리고 한식집에서 전통 음식을 드시는 할아버지, 할머니들을 볼 수 있습니다. 이렇게 인사동에는 볼거리[9]와 먹거리[10]가 많아서 나이 어린 학생들부터 할아버지, 할머니까지 그리고 외국인들도 모두 자주 가는 곳입니다. 한국의 전통 문화의 중심지[11]인 인사동은 서울에서 꼭 가 볼 만한[12] 곳입니다.

1. 전통 문화: traditional culture
2. 맛보다: to taste
3. ~까지 이르다: reach up to
4. 거리: street, avenue
5. 공예품: craftwork
6. 골동품: antique
7. 화랑: gallery
8. 전통 찻집: traditional teahouse
9. 볼거리: things to watch
10. 먹거리: things to eat
11. 중심지: center (of)
12. ~(으)ㄹ 만한: worthy of

USAGE

1 Using postal services

(1) (Sending mail and packages at the post office)

A: 소포 부치려고 하는데요.

B: 어디 보내실 거예요?

A: 부산에 보내려고요.

B: 보통으로 하실래요, 등기로 하실래요?

A: 보통으로 해 주세요.

(2) (Buying something at the post office)

손님: 우표 10장 주세요.

우체국 직원: 얼마짜리 드릴까요?

손님: 340원짜리로 주세요. 참, 엽서는 한 장에 얼마예요?

우체국 직원: 한 장에 650원입니다.

손님: 그럼, 세 장 주세요.

우체국 직원: 여기 있습니다.

손님: 전부(all) 얼마예요?

우체국 직원: 5,350원입니다.

You may hear the following expressions from a postal clerk.

우체국 직원: 몇 장 드릴까요?/필요하세요?

여기 있어요.

(소포) 어디 보내실 거예요?

소포 안에 뭐 들어 있어요?

Useful words

우편 mail service, 우편 번호 a postal code, 우편 요금 postage, 엽서 a postcard, 봉투 an envelope, 주소 an address, 답장('a reply')을 쓰다/보내다, 우표를 붙이다 to put a stamp on, 소포를 찾다 to pick up a package

Exercise 1

Practice the following conversation. (Mark wants to borrow a stamp and an envelope from his roommate Woojin.)

마크: 우진 씨, 미안하지만 <u>우표</u> 있으면 한 장 주실래요?
우진: 네, 있어요. 드릴게요.
마크: 참, <u>봉투</u>도 있으면 한 장 주세요.
우진: <u>봉투</u>는 없는데요.

Practice the above conversation again, substituting the following for the underlined parts.

(1) 엽서   (2) 편지 봉투

Exercise 2

Practice the following dialogue.

마크: 민지 씨, 어디 가세요?
민지: <u>우표 사러</u> 우체국에 가는 길이에요.
마크: 잘 됐네요. 그럼 우체국에서 이 편지 좀 부쳐 주실래요?
민지: 네, 그러죠.
마크: 고맙습니다.
민지: 뭘요. 가는 길인데요.

Take the roles of 마크 and 민지. Change the underlined parts above with the following expressions and practice the conversation again.

(1) 소포(를) 부치다
(2) 엽서(를) 사다
(3) 생일 카드(를) 보내다
(4) 소포(를) 찾다

Exercise 3

You are in Seoul and want to mail a postcard (엽서) to your friend at Jeju University. You need to find out the postage and the postal code (우편 번호). Complete the following dialogue between a postal clerk and you.

You:	이 엽서 제주도에 보내려고 하는데요.
	_____?
직원:	340원짜리 두 장 붙이시면 돼요.
You:	_____?
직원:	이삼 일 정도 걸립니다.
You:	_____?
직원:	잠깐만 기다려 보세요.
	제주 대학 우편 번호는 690-756입니다.

Exercise 4

(Role-play) Take the roles of a postal clerk and a customer for the following situations:

(1) A customer wants to buy ten 250-won stamps.
(2) A customer wants to buy five envelopes.
(3) A customer wants to mail a package containing a book to Sydney.

Notes

2   *Giving a warning and seeking advice*

(1) 직원: 손님, 포장(packing)을 이렇게 하시면 안 돼요.

    손님: 그럼, 어떻게 해야 돼요?

    직원: 상자에 담아서 테이프(tape)로 잘 붙이셔야죠.

    손님: 네, 알겠습니다.

(2) 선생님: 수업 시간에 영어를 쓰면 안 돼요.

    학생: 그럼 모르는 게 있으면 어떻게 해야 돼요?

    선생님: 수업이 끝나고 영어로 물어 보세요.

    학생: 네, 알겠습니다.

(3) A: 주말에 소포를 보내려면 어느 우체국에 가야 돼요?

    B: 중앙 우체국에 가셔야지요.

    A: 중앙 우체국에 가려면 몇 번 버스를 타야 돼요?

    B: 480번을 타세요.

    A: 미국에 엽서를 보내려면 얼마짜리 우표를 붙여야 돼요?

    B: 400원짜리(worth)를 붙이세요.

When giving advice or a warning, the negative conditional form ~(으)면 안 되다 'You shouldn't . . . , Please don't . . . '(*Lit.*, 'If you do . . . , it is not good'.) is often used, as illustrated below.

수업 시간에 영어를   A Korean language teacher tells students
쓰면 안 됩니다.   not to use English during class.

손님, 포장을 이렇게   A postal clerk gives a customer advice
하시면 안 됩니다.   on wrapping packages.

For seeking advice, you can say 그럼, 어떻게 해야 돼요? 'Then, what should I do?/What am I supposed to do?' To express an opinion or to give advice, ~어/아야지요 'should, ought to' is often used. For example, at a post office, a customer is about to leave without taking his/her change.

Clerk: 손님, 거스름돈 받아 가셔야지요.
Customer: 아, 네. 고맙습니다.

Exercise 2

Give your opinion or advice for the following situations.

(1) 한국어를 잘하고 싶어요.

(2) 아르바이트를 하고 싶은데 어떻게 찾아요?

(3) 숙제를 하기 싫을 때는 어떻게 해야 돼요?

(~기 싫다 'to hate to do . . .')

(4) 몸이 아플 때 어떻게 해요?

(5) 싼 비행기 표를 사고 싶은데 어떻게 하는 게 좋을까요?

(6) 좋은 친구를 사귀고 싶어요.

3 *Writing personal letters*

Read the following letter and answer the questions.

그리운 어머니께,

그동안 안녕하셨어요? 할머니, 아버지께서도 안녕하시지요? 저도 몸 건강히 잘 지내고 있습니다. 먼저 어머니의 생신을 축하 드립니다. 여기 작은 선물을 보냅니다. 어머니께서 좋아하시는 빨간 색 옷을 샀습니다. 어머니 마음에 드셨으면 좋겠어요.

이 곳은 이제 또 새 학기가 시작되어 바빠지기 시작했습니다. 어서 이번 학기를 끝내고 미국으로 돌아가고 싶습니다. 식구들도 보고 싶고, 어머니께서 만드신 맛있는 음식도 먹고 싶습니다. 누나하고 형한테도 제 안부 전해 주세요. 그럼 또 편지 쓰겠습니다. 안녕히 계세요.

2020년 8월 30일
서울에서
우진 올림

Exercise 1

Reading comprehension

(1) What present did Woojin buy for his mother?

(2) List all of Woojin's family members.

(3) How did Woojin describe his recent life in Korea?

(4) What did Woojin wish to do?

Exercise 2

Imagine that you are sending a birthday present to your friend in Korea. Write a letter to her/him.

Notes

. . . .

. . . .

. . . .

. . . .

. . . .

. . . .

Lesson 4 Life in Korea I

CONVERSATION 1   *I am on my way to Insadong*

By chance, Minji met Woojin at the dormitory's entrance.

Minji:	Woojin, where are you going?
Woojin:	I am on my way to Insadong to buy a present.
Minji:	Why?
Woojin:	Because my mom's birthday is at the end of this month.
Minji:	Oh, is that so? What are you going to buy?
Woojin:	I am thinking of buying a set of spoons and chopsticks.
Minji:	That is a good idea. If you go to Insadong, you will be able to buy something you like because it has many Korean traditional crafts shops.
Woojin:	If you happen to have time now, will you go together with me?
Minji:	Okay, I will, but I have to withdraw money from the bank on our way there.
Woojin:	Okay, you can do that.

CONVERSATION 2   *I would like to send a package.*

Woojin went to the post office in order to send a package to the United States.

Clerk:	Welcome. How can I help you?
Woojin:	How long does it take if I send a package to the United States?
Clerk:	Where in the United States?
Woojin:	New York.
Clerk:	It takes about three days.
Woojin:	Is that so? It sounds good.
Clerk:	What is inside the package? Is it fragile?
Woojin:	It is not. It is a set of spoons and chopsticks.
Clerk:	(Giving him a paper) If you want to send a package, please write the address here.
Woojin:	Okay, here it is. Thank you for your help. (Woojin leaves.)
Clerk:	Excuse me, hold on. You should take the receipt.
Woojin:	Oh, yes. Thank you.

NARRATION *Woojin's letter*

Dear Mom whom I miss,

How have you been so far? I am doing well and am in good health. First of all, happy birthday, Mom. I bought you a pretty set of spoons and chopsticks from Korea. I hope you will like them.

You must have worried about me a lot, since I didn't answer the phone the last time you called me. At that time, I was studying at the library all day long. It turned out that I will receive a scholarship because my grades were very good this semester. You don't have to send me tuition. I have gotten used to school life and have made many friends. So please don't worry about me. And please always be healthy. I miss all my family. I will write you again soon. Goodbye.

June 30, 2020
From Woojin in Seoul

CULTURE *Insadong*

If you want to taste Korean traditional culture and food, you have to go to Insadong without fail. Insadong is a street reaching from Anguk Station to Jongno 2-ga in Seoul. You can take the subway line 3 and get off at Anguk Station and walk to Insadong.

There are many antique and crafts stores and also many galleries, traditional teahouses, and traditional restaurants as well. Walking on the Insadong street, you can see students examining the craft items, foreigners buying merchandise, college students who date at the teahouse, and old men and women who eat Korean traditional food at the Korean restaurants. In other words, Insadong is a place where people of all sorts—such as young students and old men and ladies and foreigners as well—often go because there are many things to see and eat. Insadong, the center of Korean traditional culture, is a place definitely worth visiting in Seoul.

5과 한국 생활 II

Lesson 5 Life in Korea II

Conversation 1 방값도 싸고 괜찮아.

Conversation 1

우진: 수빈아, 잘 지냈어?G5.1

수빈: 응, 잘 지냈어.

우진: 혹시 괜찮은 원룸 알면 소개 좀 해 줄래?

수빈: 왜? 이사하려고?

우진: 응, 원룸으로 옮기고 싶어.

수빈: 지금 사는 아파트가 불편해?

우진: 아니. 교통도 편하고 집주인도 친절한데
방 값이 좀 비싼 편이라서.G5.2 학교 앞 원룸들 어때?

수빈: 내 친구 하나가 학교 앞 원룸에 사는데
방 값도 싸고 괜찮은 것 같아.

우진: 아, 그럼, 학교 앞 원룸을 알아봐야겠네. 그런데,
수빈아, 가구를 사려는데 어디가 싼지 알아?G5.3

수빈: 글쎄, 잘 모르겠는데. 친구들한테 한번 물어볼게.

COMPREHENSION QUESTIONS

1. 우진이는 왜 이사하려고 합니까?
2. 우진이는 어떤 방을 찾고 있습니까?
3. 우진이는 무엇을 사고 싶어합니까?

NEW WORDS

NOUN

가구	furniture
가구점	furniture store
거실	living room
배달	delivery
사무실	office
소개(하다)	introduction
아주머니	middle-aged woman
옷장	wardrobe, closet
원룸	studio apartment
주인	owner
책장	bookshelf, bookcase
침대	bed
침실	bedroom
통화(하다)	phone call
하숙방	a room in a boardinghouse
하숙비	boarding expenses
하숙집	boardinghouse

PRONOUN

너	you (plain form)

VERB

구하다	to search for
벗다	to take off
옮기다	to move, shift

ADJECTIVE

부족하다	to be insufficient

ADVERB

반드시	surely, certainly

SUFFIX

~(으)ㄴ/는 편이다	to tend to
~(으)ㄴ/는지 알다/모르다	to know/not know whether
~어/아	intimate speech style
아/야	vocative suffix

INTERJECTION

응	yeah

NEW EXPRESSIONS

1. In 수빈아, the plain-level vocative particle 아 is attached at the end of someone's first name to draw the attention of the addressee in a discourse context. The particle 아 is attached after a name that ends with a consonant (e.g., 수빈아); after a name that ends with a vowel, the particle 야 is used instead (e.g., 민지야).

These particles are typically used to address a child by another child or an adult; they are also used to address an adult by his or her parents or by a friend whose friendship began in childhood.

2. 혹시 'by any chance, in case, possibly' is used often in a conditional sentence or in a question.

3. 옮기다 and 이사하다 are used interchangeably in the text but, there are some differences between the two. 이사하다 means basically 'to move one's residence' while 옮기다 has the wider range of meanings 'to move (things), transfer, translate' and 'to infect (with disease)'.

4. 사려는데 is a contracted form of 사려고 하는데. 고 하 is omitted in other constructions as in 사려면 (from 사려고 하면 'if you want to buy').

Grammar

G5.1   The intimate speech style ~어/아

(1) 마크: 여보세요.

   동수: 마크, 나**야**.   Mark, it's me. Did you call
        아까 전화했**어**?   me a little while ago?

   마크: 응, 혹시 내일 등산 **갈 거야**?

   동수: 응, 왜? 너도 같이 갈**래**?

(2) 마크: 응. 그럼, 내일 아침에 전화할**까**?

   동수: 그러지 말고, 그냥 아침에 우리 집으로 **와**.

   마크: 응, 알았**어**.

(3) A: 지금 사는 하숙집 어**때**?

   B: 하숙비도 싸고 가구가 있어서 편**해**.
        침대랑 옷장도 있고 책장도 두 개나 있**어**.

Examples

Notes

1. Between close people, e.g., friends from childhood, siblings, etc., the so-called intimate (speech) style is used. The intimate style is represented by the ending ~어/아.

2. Note that the polite style ~어요/아요 consists of the intimate style ending ~어/아 followed by the polite marker ~요. Therefore, the intimate style is subject to the same variation as the polite ~어요/아요 style. That is, the form is ~아 if the last vowel of the verb stem is either 아 or 오, as in 좋아, except that the ending ~아 is deleted if the stem ends in 아 or 애 without a final consonant, as in 가. Otherwise the form is ~어, as in 있어. When the predicate is -하다, 하+어 renders 해, as in 편해 in (3) (cf. 편해요). After the past-tense marker ~었/았, ~어 is used regardless of the stem vowel.

Note also the following variations.

After the copula 이, ~야 is attached, as in 나야 in (1):

| 저예요 | → | 나야 |
| 갈 거예요 | → | 갈 거야 |

When the stem ends in 오, as in 오다, the stem and the intimate ending are contracted to 와, as in (2):

| 오+아 | → | 와 |

For other endings, the intimate style is made by deleting the polite marker ~요 from the polite style, as in 어때 in (3): cf. 어때요.

	Dictionary form	Polite style	Intimate style	~었/았-	~(으)ㄹ래
~아	이다	이에요/예요	(이)야	이었어/였어	*
	좋다	좋아요	좋아	좋았어	*
	작다	작아요	작아	작았어	*
	찾다	찾아요	찾아	찾았어	찾을래
	가다	가요	가	갔어	갈래
~어	있다	있어요	있어	있었어	있을래
	쉬다	쉬어요	쉬어	쉬었어	쉴래
Contracted	보다	봐요	봐	봤어	볼래
	오다	와요	와	왔어	올래
	어렵다	어려워요	어려워	어려웠어	*
	쉽다	쉬워요	쉬워	쉬웠어	*
	전화하다	전화해요	전화해	전화했어	전화할래
	되다	돼요	돼	됐어	될래

[* indicates that the form is not available because of the semantic nature of the predicate. Adjectives cannot be used with the intention suffix ~(으)ㄹ래 because intention requires an action.]

3. When the intimate speech style is used, expressions such as 'yes' and 'no' must be switched to non-polite forms as in (1) and (2):

네/예 → 응
아니요 → 아니

Exercises

Convert the given dialogue into the intimate speech style.

(1) A: 어디까지 가세요? → <u>어디까지 가?</u>

B: 관악역까지 가요. → <u>관악역까지 가.</u>

(2) A: 가게 주인 아주머니는 어디 가셨어요?

B: 물건 배달 가셨는데요. 왜요?

(3) A: 왜 요즘 그렇게 연락을 안 했어요?

B: 미안해요. 좀 바빴거든요.

(4) A: 저 사람은 누구예요?

B: 아마 린다 동생일 거예요.

(5) A: 하숙방은 구하셨어요?

B: 아니요, 아직 알아보고 있어요.

G5.2 ~(으)ㄴ/는 편이다 'it is more the case of . . . than the other'

Examples

(1) A: 새로 이사간 아파트 어때?

B: 침실은 작지만 거실이 넓**은 편이야**.

(2) A: 요즘 부모님 건강이 어떠세요?

B: 건강하**신 편이에요**.   They are on the healthy side.

(3) A: 보통 몇 시에 주무세요?

B: 늦게 자**는 편이에요**.

(4) A: 서울 물가가 어때요?

B: 도쿄(Tokyo)보다는 싸지만 비**싼 편이에요**.

(5) A: 골프 자주 치는 **편이에요**?

B: 아니요, 골프 안 쳐요.

Notes

1. 편 literally means 'a side, a group, a team', as in

> 우리 편 'our team'   상대편 'the opponent'
>
> 이 편 'this side'   저 편 'that side' or 'the other side'

2. ~(으)ㄴ/는 편이다, literally meaning 'It belongs to the side of . . .', is an expression of approximation that gives the effect of saying 'I cannot say this or that, but if you ask me to choose one way or the other, I would say it is more this way than the other'.

3. As noun-modifying forms, ~(으)ㄴ 편이다 is used for adjectives and ~는 편이다 for verbs.

Exercises

Using ~(으)ㄴ/는 편이에요, answer the following questions.

(1) A: 골프 자주 치세요?

B: 네, 일주일에 두 번 치니까 <u>자주 치는 편이에요</u>.

(2) 소연: 새로 이사 간 동네 어때?

성희: 응, 좋아. 슈퍼마켓도 가깝고 교통도 _____

(3) 성희: 스티브 씨, 영화 보는 거 좋아해요?

스티브: _____

특히 코미디를 좋아해요.

(4) A: 음악회 자주 가세요?

B: 네, 요즘은 잘 못 가지만 _____

한 달에 한 번 정도 가요.

(5) 소연: 성희야, 왜 백화점에 안 가고 여기 왔어?

성희: 여기가 백화점보다 _____

(6) 성희: 소연아, 하루에 몇 시간 자?

소연: _____

하루에 5시간밖에 못 자서 항상 잠이 부족해.

G5.3	~(으)ㄴ/는지 알다/모르다 'know/don't know whether (what, who, where, when) . . .'

Verb~는지:

(1) 우진: 민지 씨, 우체국이
   어디 있**는지 아세요?**

   Minji, do you know where the post office is?

   민지: 네, 알아요.

(2) 한국에서는 방에서 반드시
   신발을 벗어야 되**는지 몰랐어요**.

Adj.~(으)ㄴ지:

(3) A: 가구를 사려고 하는데
   어디가 제일 싼**지 아세요?**

   B: 은행 앞에 있는 가구점이
   제일 싸요.

N~(이)ㄴ지:

(4) A: 오늘이 무슨 날**인지 아세요?**

   B: 아니요, 무슨 날인데요?

   A: 제 생일이에요.

~었는지/았는지:

(5) 우진: 샌디 씨, 작년에 한국어를
   누가 가르쳤**는지 아세요?**

   Sandy, do you know who taught Korean last year?

   샌디: 네, 이 선생님께서 가르치셨어요.

(6) A: 어제가 무슨 날이었**는지 아세요?**

   B: 한글날(Hangul Day)이요.

(7) A: 스티브 아직 한국에 있어요?

   B: 저는 스티브가 한국에 갔**는지도 몰랐어요**.

Notes

1. ~(으)ㄴ/는지 introduces an indirect question. It occurs with question words such as 어디 (where), 무엇 (what), 무슨 (which . . . , what kind of . . .), 누구/누가 (who), 어떻게 (how), 얼마나 (how much/many), 언제 (when), 왜 (why), etc., and is followed by either 알다 or 모르다.

2. In the non-past tense, it shows the same variation in conjugation of predicate as noun-modifying forms; that is, verbs take ~는지, whereas adjectives and the copula -이 take ~(으)ㄴ지 and ~(이)ㄴ지, respectively.

In the past tense, on the other hand, it is ~었는지/았는지 regardless of predicate types.

	~(으)ㄴ/는지		Noun-modifying forms	
	Non-past	Past	Non-past	Past
Verb	~는지	~었는지	~는	~(으)ㄴ/던
Adjective	~(으)ㄴ지	~었/았는지	~(으)ㄴ	~던
Copula	~(이)ㄴ지	~이었는지	~(이)ㄴ	~(이)던

Exercises

1. Fill in the blanks using the appropriate forms of ~(으)ㄴ/는지.

(1) 민지가 왜 기분이 (좋다)_____ 알아?
    지금 남자 친구랑 통화하고 있거든.

(2) 김 교수님 어디 (계시다) _____알아요?
    아마 사무실에 계실 거예요.

(3) 기숙사가 왜 이렇게 (조용하다)_____ 아세요?
    학생들이 모두 집으로 돌아갔거든요.

(4) 상자에 뭐가 (들어있다) _____ 알아요?
    지난 학기에 쓰던 책이요.

2. Ask your classmates the following questions using the ~는지/(으)ㄴ지
아세요? 'Do you know . . . ?'

(1) Who invented the Korean alphabet (Hangul)?

(2) When is Hangul Day?

(3) How many days are there in May?

(4) Where is the closest post office?

(5) When is the final exam for Korean class this term?

(6) What language do they speak in Chile?

(7) Who is the richest man in America?

(8) Why did John not come to school yesterday?

(Variation) Go around the classroom and find the person who knows the answer.

Notes

. . . .

. . . .

. . . .

. . . .

. . . .

. . . .

Conversation 2   이사 온 지 얼마나 됐어요?

▌ 스티브가 새로 이사 온 하숙집에서 에이미와 이야기합니다.

Conversation   2

스티브: 안녕하세요. 2층에 새로 이사 온 스티브입니다.

에이미: 아, 네. 안녕하세요. 저는 에이미예요.

　　　　　이사 온 지 얼마나 되셨어요?[G5.4]

스티브: 어제 이사 왔어요.

에이미: 그럼 짐 정리도 아직 안 됐겠네요.

스티브: 대충 됐는데 인터넷 연결이 잘 안 되네요.

에이미: 아, 그래요? 그럼 PC방에 가 보세요.

　　　　　돈을 내고 인터넷을 사용할 수 있어요.

스티브: 아, 그런 곳이 있어요?

에이미: 네, 한국에는 가게들 이름이 무슨무슨 방이 많아요.

　　　　　PC방, 노래방, 만화방, 그리고 찜질방도 있어요.

스티브: 찜질방은 뭐 하는 데예요?

에이미: 목욕도 하고 사우나도 하고 쉬기도 하는 곳이에요.

스티브: 재미있네요.

에이미: 공부하다가[G5.5] 힘들면 한번 가 보세요.

　　　　　스트레스도 풀 수 있어서 좋아요.

COMPREHENSION QUESTIONS

1. 스티브는 하숙집으로 언제 이사 왔습니까?
2. PC방은 어떤 곳입니까?
3. 찜질방은 어떤 곳입니까?

NEW WORDS

NOUN

냉장고	refrigerator
만화방	comic book rental store
사우나	sauna
사투리	dialect
세탁기	washing machine
소파	sofa
식탁	dining table
아르바이트	part-time job
연결(하다)	connection, link
운전 면허	driver's license
정리(하다)	arrangement
지갑	wallet
지방	region, district
찜질방	Korean dry sauna
청소기	vacuum cleaner
피시방	Internet café

VERB

눕다	to lie down
돌아가다	to return (to)
사귀다	② to date
사용하다	to use
잠이 들다	to fall asleep
헤어지다	to break up

ADJECTIVE

그립다	to miss, long for

ADVERB

대충	roughly
방금	a moment ago

SUFFIX

~(으)ㄴ/는 지 [ ] 되다	It has been [time span] since . . .
~다가	movement from one action/state to another

NEW EXPRESSIONS

1. 되 vs. 돼

Because the pronunciations are almost identical, this is a source for misspelling for both native speakers and foreign learners. 되 is a stem form, while 돼 is a combination of 되 + ~어 as shown below.

됩니다   돼요 (= 되어요) 되면
돼서 (= 되어서) 되는
되지만   됐어요 (= 되었어요)
               됐는데 (= 되었는데)

2. In 무슨무슨 방, speakers duplicate the indefinite pronoun 무슨 'something, some kind of' to be used as an expression like "such and such".

Grammar

G5.4   A: ~(으)ㄴ 지 얼마나 됐어요? 'How long has it been since . . . ?'
B: ~(으)ㄴ 지 TIME SPAN(이/가) 됐어요. 'It has been . . . since . . .'

(1) 소연: 한국에 **오신 지**   How long has it been since you
얼마나 됐어요?   came to Korea?

마크: (한국에 **온 지) 이제**   Now it's been half a year (since I
반 년 됐는데 벌써   came to Korea), and I already miss
친구들이 그리워요.   my friends.

(2) A: 운전면허 받**은 지 얼마나 됐어요?**

B: 1년 됐어요.

(3) A: 점심 먹으러 갈래요?

B: 벌써요? 아침 먹**은 지 2시간밖에 안 됐어요**.

(4) A: 백화점에서 뭐 사셨어요?

B: 냉장고하고 청소기요.
이사온 **지 하루밖에 안 돼서** 필요한 게 많거든요.

(5) 동수는 지방에서 서울로 **온 지** 벌써 2년이나 됐는데
아직도 사투리를 써요.

Notes

1. TIME SPAN(이/가) 되다 indicates the amount of time that has passed since a certain time.

2. ~(으)ㄴ 지 TIME SPAN(이/가) 되다 expresses the amount of time that has elapsed since the event at issue took place. The reference event is expressed in ~(으)ㄴ 지. It can best be translated as 'It has been [TIME SPAN] since . . .' or '[TIME SPAN] has passed since . . .' The question asking about the time lapse is made with the question word 얼마나, hence ~(으)ㄴ 지 얼마나 됐어요? 'How long has it been since . . . ?'

3. TIME SPAN이/가 되다 is typically in the past tense form.

Exercises

Make up dialogues based on the given information, following the pattern as in (1).

(1) [민지는 3년 전에 피아노를 배우기 시작했습니다.]
    우진: <u>민지 씨, 피아노 배운 지 얼마나 됐어요?</u>
    민지: <u>3년 됐어요.</u>

(2) [스티브는 6개월 전에 미국으로 돌아갔습니다.]
    민지: _____
    스티브: _____

(3) [동수는 지난 주에 새 지갑을 선물 받았습니다.]
    소연: _____
    동수: _____

(4) [지나는 1년 전에 아르바이트를 시작했습니다.]
    성희: _____
    지나: _____

(5) [성희는 4달 전에 하숙집에서 살기 시작했습니다.]
    소연: _____
    성희: _____

(6) [소연이는 3일 전에 새 냉장고하고 세탁기를 샀습니다.]
    성희: _____
    소연: _____

G5.5 ~다가: transference of an action/state to another

(1) 스티브는 그동안 아파트에서 살**다가** 학교 앞 하숙집으로 옮겼습니다.

During that time, Steve had lived in an apartment and then moved to a 하숙집 that is in front of his school.

(2) 동수는 수잔이랑 사귀**다가** 작년에 헤어졌어요.

Dongsoo and Susan had been dating but then broke up last year.

(3) 마크는 학교에서 나오**다가** 샌디를 만났어요.

On his way coming out of school, Mark met Sandy.

(4) 민지가 소파에 누워 있**다가** 방금 잠이 들었어요.

While lying down on a sofa, Minji fell asleep a moment ago.

Notes

1. The suffix ~다가 indicates that momentum is transferred from one action or state to another; that is, a person or an object engaged in an action or a state of affairs turns to another action or state.

2. ~다가 indicates a shift, but one that takes place only after the earlier action has been completed as in (1) and (2). It may be translated as '. . . was (engaged in) ~ing, then . . .'

3. ~다가 is also used to indicate that a new action or state occurs in the middle of the first action or state; that is, the first action has not reached its end point as in (3) and (4). It may be variously translated as 'in the middle of ~ing', 'while ~ing', 'on the way to . . .'

![Exercise]

Exercise

1. Describe what happened while you were engaged in the given action.

    (1) On my way home: <u>집에 오다가 스티브를 만났어요</u>.

    (2) On the way to school: _____

    (3) While playing basketball: _____

    (4) I was dozing off during the class: _____

    (5) I was going shopping: _____

2. Say in Korean what you would do when the situation specified in parentheses occurs while you are engaged in the given situation.

    (1) I am studying. (피곤해지다)

        <u>공부하다가 피곤해지면 나가서 운동을 해요</u>.

    (2) I am on my way back home. (배가 고프다)

        _____

    (3) I am sleeping. (목이 마르다)

        _____

    (4) I am driving. (졸리다)

        _____

    (5) I am eating. (배가 아프다)

        _____

3. Describe how your earlier action has changed.

    (1) 한국에서 공부하다가 <u>지난 달에 미국으로 돌아왔어요</u>.

    (2) 2년 동안 일하다가 _____

    (3) 여름 방학에 쉬다가 _____

    (4) 매일 햄버거만 먹다가 _____

    (5) 두 학기 동안 한국어를 배우다가 _____

    (6) 룸메이트하고 같이 살다가 _____

    (7) 항상 콜라만 마시다가 _____

Narration	스티브의 하숙방

스티브가 한국에 온 지도 벌써 6개월이 됐습니다. 스티브는 그동안 학교 기숙사에서 살다가 지난 주말에 학교 앞 하숙집으로 옮겼습니다. 하숙집은 방은 작지만 주인 아주머니가 아주 친절하시고 하숙비도 싼 편입니다. 또한, 하숙집은 아침과 저녁을 주기 때문에 점심만 학교에서 사 먹으면 됩니다.

스티브의 하숙방은 온돌[1]방입니다. 침대는 없고, 책상과 책장, 그리고 작은 옷장이 있습니다. 온돌방은 바닥[2]이 따뜻해서 추운 겨울에도 바닥에서 잘 수 있습니다. 스티브는 처음에는 온돌방이 불편했지만, 이제는 미국에 돌아가면 온돌방이 그리울 것 같습니다.

1. 온돌: floor heating system   2. 바닥: floor

▶▶ COMPREHENSION QUESTIONS

1. 스티브는 하숙집으로 이사오기 전에 어디서 살았습니까?
2. 새로 이사온 하숙집은 어떻습니까?
3. 스티브 방 안에는 어떤 가구가 있습니까?
4. 온돌방은 무엇이 좋습니까?

NEW EXPRESSIONS

아주머니, a kinship term for 'aunt', is used here to refer to a middle-aged woman.

Notes

CULTURE

하숙과 자취

한국의 대학생들은 보통 부모님과 같이 삽니다. 그런데 집하고 학교가 먼 경우[1]
에는 학교 근처에서 하숙이나 자취[2]를 하기도 합니다. 하숙은 집 주인에게
방값과 식비[3]를 내고 주인 집에서 먹고 자는 경우를 말합니다. 주인 아주머니가
보통 아침과 저녁 식사를 준비해 줍니다. 하숙집에서 다른 하숙생들과 생활하기
때문에 친구들도 많이 사귈 수 있고 외롭지[4] 않아서 좋습니다.

하숙 생활이 불편한 학생들은 자취를 합니다. 자취는 직접 밥도 하고 빨래와
청소를 하면서 사는 경우입니다. 주인 집에서 방만 빌리는 경우도 있고
오피스텔이나 원룸과 같은 곳을 빌리는 경우도 있습니다. 한국의 '원룸'은 미국의
studio를 말합니다. 오피스텔은 오피스와 호텔을 줄인[5] 말입니다. 낮에는 일을
하거나 공부를 하고 밤에는 잠을 자는 곳입니다. 원룸이나 오피스텔 생활이
편리하기 때문에 요즘은 직장인[6]들도 원룸과 오피스텔에서 많이 삽니다.

1. 경우: case
2. 자취(하다): to live on one's own
3. 식비: food expenses
4. 외롭다: to be lonely
5. 줄이다: to shorten
6. 직장인: office worker

Examples

USAGE

1 *Searching for housing*

(1) 성희: 마크 씨, 지금 어디 사세요?

마크: 학교 근처 아파트에 살고 있어요.

성희: 그래요? 아파트가 좋아요?

마크: 괜찮아요. 동네도 조용하고 교통도 편리하고 건물도 깨끗해요. 성희 씨 지금 살고 있는 아파트는 어때요?

성희: 방도 넓고 다 좋은데, 방 값이 좀 비싸요.

마크: 얼마예요?

성희: 한 달에 800불이에요.

(2) A: 요즘 방 보러 다니는 중이에요.

B: 어떤 방을 구하세요(looking for)?

A: 교통이 편리하고 방이 넓고 깨끗했으면 좋겠어요.

B: 신문 광고(advertisement) 보셨어요?

A: 네, 그런데 아직 좋은 걸 못 찾았어요.

Exercise 1

Converse with your partner about the following questions.

(1) 지금 어디 사세요? (아파트, 기숙사, 하숙집, etc.)

(2) 한 달에 방값이 얼마예요?

(3) 언제 방값을 내야 돼요?

(4) 빨래는 보통 어디서 해요?

(5) 교통이 편리해요?

Exercise 2

Take different roles to practice the following conversation.

A: 요즘 아파트 보러 다니는 중이에요.

B: 어떤 방을 찾으세요?

A: 교통이 편리하고 방이 넓고 깨끗했으면 좋겠어요.

B: 신문 광고 보셨어요?

A: 네. 그런데 좋은 아파트는 너무 비싸요.

Substitute the underlined part above with the following:

(1) You want to rent a quiet studio near your school.

(2) You want to rent an apartment in a safe neighborhood.

(3) You want to rent a room with a private bathroom in a nice house.

Exercise 3

Draw a line from each question to an appropriate answer between a prospective tenant and a landlord. Then practice with your partner.
독방 'a single room'

실례합니다. 주인 계십니까? •   • 마침 방이 하나 있어요.

독방 있어요?   •   • 전데요. 어떻게 오셨어요?

하숙비는 어떻게 돼요?   •   • 방 옆에 있어요.

이번 주말에 이사해도 돼요? •   • 한 달에 삼십만 원이에요.

화장실은 어디 있어요?   •   • 화장실에 세탁기가 있어요.

빨래는 어디서 해요?   •   • 네, 그럼요.

2 *Describing buildings and interiors*

소연:	어머, 이 <u>책상</u> 참 좋네요. 어디서 사셨어요?
스티브:	신문 광고 보고 샀어요. 중고품[1]이에요.
소연:	꼭 새 거 같이 보이는데, 이게 중고 가구[2]예요?
스티브:	네, 저도 중고 가구점에 가서 보고 놀랐어요[3].
소연:	싸게 샀겠네요. 얼마 주셨어요?
스티브:	20불 줬어요.
소연:	와, 정말 싸네요.

1. 중고품: used merchandise
2. 중고 가구: used furniture
3. 놀라다: to be surprised

Exercise 3

Practice the conversation above again, substituting the following for 책상.

(1) 텔레비전

(2) 책장

(3) 식탁

(4) 소파

(5) 냉장고

Notes

Exercise 2

Read the following letter that Steve wrote to his teacher in New York and
answer the questions.

이민수 선생님께,

　선생님, 그동안 안녕하셨습니까? 제가 한국에 온 지도 벌써 반년이
됐습니다. 저는 그동안 학교 근처 아파트에 살다가 지난 주 토요일에
하숙집으로 이사했습니다. 아파트에 살 때는 매일 밥을 해 먹는 게
힘들었는데, 새로 이사한 하숙집에서는 아침, 저녁 식사를 다 주니까 참
편리합니다. 하숙집 음식도 맛있고 주인 아주머니도 아주 친절합니다.
미국에 다시 돌아갈 때까지 계속 이 하숙집에서 살려고 합니다. 좋은
방을 찾기도 힘들고, 또 이사를 하기도 쉽지 않기 때문입니다.

　제가 지금 살고 있는 하숙집은 온돌방입니다. 방안에는 책상, 옷장,
컴퓨터, 책장이 두 개 있습니다. 하숙집은 학교까지 걸어서 20분 정도
걸립니다. 이 곳에 사는 하숙생들은 거의 다 저하고 같은 학교에 다니는
대학생들입니다. 중국에서 온 남학생도 한 명 있습니다. 하숙집 앞에는
작은 슈퍼도 있고 또 찜질방이 있어서 참 편리합니다.

그럼 또 연락 드리겠습니다. 거기 한국어 반 친구들한테 안부 전해
주십시오.

2020년 9월 12일
서울에서
스티브 올림

Mark T(rue) or F(alse) for the following statements.

(1) _____ Steve came to Korea a year ago.
(2) _____ Steve used to live in a dormitory in Seoul.
(3) _____ The boardinghouse does not offer lunch.
(4) _____ Steve plans to stay in the same house until graduation.
(5) _____ Steve does not have a bed in his room.
(6) _____ It takes only ten minutes from Steve's place to school.

Useful words

안방 the master bedroom, 화장실 a bathroom, 부엌 a kitchen, 거실 a living room, 공부방 a study room, 현관 the entrance, 차고 a garage, 마당/정원 a yard, 이층 the second floor, 일층 the first floor, 아래층 the downstairs, 수영장 a swimming pool

가구 furniture, 침대 a bed, 책상 a desk, 의자 a chair, 사진 a photo, 세탁기 a washer, 옷장/장롱 a closet, 서랍 a drawer, 냉장고 a refrigerator, 소파 a sofa, 램프 a lamp, 그릇 a dish, 식탁 a dining table, 청소기 a vacuum cleaner

Exercise 3

Write a letter to one of your friends describing the apartment (including furniture) or house you live in.

2 Initiating a conversation and introducing oneself

Examples

(1) 소연: 혹시 스티브 씨 아니세요?

스티브: 네, 그런데요.

소연: 저 성희 친구 최소연이에요. 성희한테서 스티브 씨 말씀 많이 들었어요.

스티브: 아, 최소연 씨세요? 저도 말씀 많이 들었습니다. 앞으로 잘 부탁 드립니다.

소연: 저도요. 반갑습니다. 여기 이사하신 지 얼마나 됐어요?

스티브: 일주일 됐어요.

(2) 영미: 저어, 실례지만 혹시 김철수 씨 아니세요?

철수: 네, 그런데요. 저를 어떻게 아세요?

영미: 나 모르겠어? 고등학교 때 같은 학교에 다녔잖아.

철수: 아, 김영미!

영미: 응! 정말 오래간만이야.

To check and confirm information, you can initiate conversation with the structure, 혹시 . . . 아니세요/아니에요? as shown above.

When you run into an acquaintance unexpectedly, you can express your surprise by saying the following

> 아니, 영미 씨 아니세요?
> 여기 웬일이세요?

 Exercise 1

(Role-play) Twenty years after you graduated from a high school, you run across your classmate at a supermarket.

 Exercise 2

Imagine that you run into your classmate from Korean classes ten years later on a subway in New York City. How would you start a conversation? Make a dialogue with your classmate. Include questions such as "How long have you been in New York?"

| 4 | *Giving compliments and responding to compliments* |

In Korean culture, it is usual for people to deny or respond in a negative way when they receive compliments from others. For example,

(1) Responding when someone praises your Korean skill

    A: 한국어 배운 지 얼마나 됐어요?
    B: 이제 일 년 됐어요.
    A: 어머, 일 년밖에 안 됐는데 한국말을 참 잘 하시네요.
    B: 뭘요('Not at all'.), 아직 많이 부족해요.

(2) Responding when someone thanks you for a present

    A: 생일 선물 감사합니다.
    B: 조그만 거예요.   'Don't mention it'. (*Lit.*, 'It is a very small thing'.)

(3) Offering food to a guest at a party

    Host: 차린 건 없지만 많이 드세요.   (*Lit.*, 'Although I didn't prepare anything, please eat a lot'.)

    Guest: 잘 먹겠습니다.

Examples

By depreciating one's Korean language skill or belittling the present or food one offers, Koreans try to express humility. The attitude of holding back or depreciating oneself is considered to be very humble (and thus polite) in Korean culture.

 Exercise 1

How would you respond to the following compliments?

   (1) 크리스마스 선물 고맙습니다.
   (2) 오늘 입은 옷 참 예쁘네요!
   (3) 그 시계 어디서 사셨어요? 아주 멋있네요.
        (멋있다 'to be stylish, attractive')
   (4) 노래를 참 잘 부르시네요!
   (5) 한국어를 참 잘 하세요.
   (6) 구두하고 옷하고 잘 어울려요.

 Exercise 2

Practice the conversation, substituting the underlined parts with the following.

   A: <u>골프 치신 지</u> 얼마나 됐어요?
   B: 이제 일 년 됐어요.
   A: 일 년밖에 안 됐는데 참 잘 하시네요.
   B: 뭘요, 아직 많이 부족해요.

   (1)   피아노를 치다
   (2)   스키를 타다
   (3)   한국어를 배우다
   (4)   테니스를 치다
   (5)   볼링 치다 (bowling)
   (6)   your own hobbies

Lesson 5 Life in Korea II

CONVERSATION 1   *It is nice with pretty cheap rent.*

Woojin:	Soobin, how are you getting along?
Soobin:	I am getting along well.
Woojin:	Will you tell me about a nice studio if you happen to know any?
Soobin:	Why? Do you want to move?
Woojin:	Yes. These days I am thinking of moving to a studio.
Soobin:	Is the apartment you are now staying at inconvenient?
Woojin:	No. It has easy access and the landlord is kind, but the rent is rather on the expensive side. How are the studios in front of the school?
Soobin:	One of my friends lives in a studio in front of the school. It seems to be nice, and the rent is pretty cheap.
Woojin:	Oh, then, I should look for a studio in front of the school. By the way, Soobin, do you know where the best place to buy furniture is?
Soobin:	I don't. I will ask my friend.

CONVERSATION 2   *How long has it been since you moved here?*

Steve talks with Amy, who lives in the boardinghouse he just moved into.

Steve:	How are you? I am Steve and just moved here.
Amy:	Oh, yes. How are you? I am Amy. How long has it been since you moved here?
Steve:	I moved here yesterday.
Amy:	Then you must have not even unpacked yet.
Steve:	I am almost done but I can't get an Internet connection.
Amy:	Is that so? Then try going to a PC room. You can pay and use the Internet.
Steve:	Oh, are there such places?
Amy:	Yes, in Korea there are many kinds of *bang* (room), such as PC room, singing room, comic book reading room, and Korean dry sauna.
Steve:	What is a Korean dry sauna for?
Amy:	It is a place where you bathe, go into a sauna, and rest.
Steve:	That's amazing.
Amy:	Try to go when you are tired from studying. It is nice because you can also release stress.

NARRATION   *Steve's room for boarding*

It has been six months since Steve came to Korea. Steve lived at the school dormitory at first and then moved to the boardinghouse in front of the school last weekend. The room at the boardinghouse is small, but the female owner is very kind, and the rent is on the cheap side. Also, since the boardinghouse provides breakfast and dinner, Steve has to buy and eat only lunch at school.

Steve's room has a floor heating system. There is no bed, but there is a desk, a bookshelf, and a small closet. People sleep on the floor in a room with a floor heating system because the floor is warm. At first, the room was uncomfortable for Steve, but it seems he will miss his room's floor heating system when he goes back to the United States.

CULTURE   하숙과 자취

Korean college students usually live with their parents. But if their home is far from school, they live in a boardinghouse or live on their own near school. In a boardinghouse you pay food expenses and room rent to the house owner and eat and sleep at the owner's house. The owner usually prepares breakfast and dinner. It is good to live in a boardinghouse because you can make many friends and you don't get lonely since you live with other students.

Students for whom a boardinghouse is inconvenient do 자취. That means that you make your own food and do your own laundry and cleaning. It can mean renting one room at someone's house or renting a place such as an officetel or studio. In Korean "one room" refers to what is called a studio in America. Officetel is a combination of the words office and hotel. It is a place where you work or study during the day and sleep at night. Many office workers also live in a studio or officetel these days because it is convenient.

6과 대중 교통

Lesson 6 Public Transportation

Conversation 1 관악산 입구에서 보자.

▶ 동수가 스티브의 핸드폰으로 전화한다.[G6.1]

Conversation 1

스티브: 어, 동수야.

동수: 스티브, 미안해.
아까는 배터리가 없어서
전화 못 받았어.

스티브: 어, 괜찮아.

동수: 무슨 일인데?

스티브: 이번 주말에 우리 관악산에
등산 가기로 했잖아.[G6.3]

동수: 응.

스티브: 그런데, 우진이는 이번 주말에 갑자기
중요한 일이 생겨서 못 갈 것 같아.

동수: 그래? 우진이도 가면 좋은데 아쉽다.[G6.2]

스티브: 할 수 없지. 그런데 우리 학교 앞에서 관악산까지
바로 가는 버스가 있어?

동수: 직접 가는 버스는 없고 중간에서 갈아타야 돼.
먼저 지하철을 타고 서울대입구역까지
간 다음 거기서 2번 버스로 갈아타면 돼.

스티브: 알았어. 그럼 이번 주 토요일 아침에
관악산 입구에서 보자.

COMPREHENSION QUESTIONS

1. 스티브가 동수 집에 전화했을 때 동수는 왜 전화를 못 받았습니까?
2. 스티브는 왜 동수한테 전화했습니까?
3. 우진이는 왜 같이 못 갑니까?
4. 학교 앞에서 관악산까지 어떻게 갑니까?
5. 스티브는 내일 동수를 어디서 만납니까?

NEW WORDS

NOUN

관악산	Gwanak Mount
남산	Nam Mount
대중	the public
배터리	battery
서울대입구역	Seoul University Station
승차권	ride pass, ticket
신호등	traffic light
약도	rough map
열쇠	key
요금	fee, fare
일기	journal
주차장	parking lot
중간	the middle
지하도	underpass

VERB

고장나다	to break down
서두르다	to hurry
세우다	to stop, pull over
잃어버리다	to lose
잡다	to catch
지키다	to guard, protect

ADJECTIVE

아쉽다	to be sorry
안전하다	to be safe
중요하다	to be important

ADVERB

바로	directly

SUFFIX

~기로 하다	decided to
~는/ㄴ다	plain speech style

NEW EXPRESSIONS

1. 관악산 is a mountain in the northeastern area of Seoul, next to 북한산 National Park. Seoul is surrounded by many beautiful mountains, and 도봉산 is one of the most popular among hikers.

2. 바로 means 'straight, directly, properly, immediately', or 'right away'. 직접 'directly, firsthand, personally' has an interchangeable usage with 바로 when used in the sense of 'directly'.

> 관악산까지 바로 가는 버스
>
> 관악산까지 직접 가는 버스

3. 버스 정류장 'a bus stop'; 기차역 'a train station'; 버스 터미널 'a bus terminal'; 택시 승차장 (= 택시 타는 곳) 'a taxi stand'.

4. 할 수 없지: the literal meaning of 할 수 없다 is 'cannot do it'. With the verb suffix ~지(요), the phrase 할 수 없지(요) is used as a fixed expression "Oh, well."

Grammar

G6.1   The plain speech style ~(는/ㄴ)다

Examples

(1) 나는 보통 7시에 아침을 먹**는다**. 그리고 8시에 학교에 간**다**.

(2) 스티브가 사는 아파트는 방이 작**다**.

(3) 스티브가 새로 이사한 집은 하숙집**이다**.
전에 살던 곳은 학교 기숙사**다**.

(4) 승차권을 잃어버려서 무료로 지하철을 **탔다**. 그래서 좀 미안**했다**.
Since I lost the subway ticket, I got a ride without a ticket. So I felt sorry.

(5) 지하철이 빠르고 안전하다. 그래서 학교 갈 때 지하철을 **탄다**.

Notes

1. The plain style is mainly used in writing such as expository writings, newspaper articles, journals, academic writing, etc.
Unlike the polite ~어요/아요 style and the deferential ~습니다 style, the plain ~(는/ㄴ)다 style does not convey politeness to the listener(s) because it is not addressed to any specific listener or reader.

2. Unlike the polite ~어요/아요 and the deferential ~습니다 styles, the plain ~(는/ㄴ)다 style has different non-past forms in verbs and adjectives. That is, verbs take ~는/ㄴ다 (~는다 after a consonant, ~ㄴ다 after a vowel) as in example (1), whereas adjectives and the copula ~이 take only ~다 as in (2) and (3). For the past tense, there is no variation between verbs and adjectives, both taking ~었/았/ㅆ다 as in (4).

3. It should be noted that there are both verbs and adjectives among ~하다 predicates. ~하다 verbs take ~는/ㄴ다 for their non-past forms, e.g., 공부한다, 하숙한다, 한국말을 한다, etc. On the other hand, ~하다 adjectives simply take ~다, as in 친절하다, 깨끗하다, etc., as in (5).

Tense marking in the plain ~다 style:

	Plain style (~다)	Polite style (~어요/아요)	Deferential style (~습니다/ㅂ니다)
Verb	~는다/ㄴ다	~어요	~습니다/ㅂ니다
Adjective	~다	~어요	~습니다/ㅂ니다
Copula	~(이)다	~이에요/예요	~입니다/ㅂ니다
Past	~었다/았다	~었/았어요	~었습니다/았습니다

Exercises

1. Convert the given sentences into the plain style.

   (1) (i)   길을 건널 때 신호등을 잘 봐야 돼요.

           → 길을 건널 때 신호등을 잘 봐야 된다.

       (ii)   스티브는 지난주 학교 앞 하숙집으로 옮겼습니다.

           → 스티브는 지난주 학교 앞 하숙집으로 옮겼다.

   (2) 집 열쇠를 잃어버려서 룸메이트를 기다리고 있어요.

   (3) 내 남자 친구는 시간을 잘 안 지켜요.

   (4) 학교 주차장이 넓어서 차를 많이 세울 수 있어요.

   (5) 한국에서는 집 안에 들어갈 때 신발을 벗고 들어갑니다.

   (6) 학교 앞에 있는 지하도로 길을 건넜어요.

   (7) 인터넷에서 새 하숙집 약도를 찾아 봤어요.

   (8) 차가 고장나서 지하철을 타고 학교에 갔습니다.

2. Convert the given narration into the polite ~어요/아요 style.

> **Example**
>
> 오늘은 민지와 함께 남산에 다녀왔다.
>
> → 오늘은 민지와 함께 남산에 다녀왔어요.

오늘은 민지와 함께 남산에 다녀왔다. 남산에 가려면 우리 학교 앞에서 지하철을 타고 명동역에서 내려서 15분쯤 걸어가면 된다. 남산 입구에 보면 케이블카 (cable car)가 있는데 왕복 요금은 7,500원, 편도는 6,000원이다. 케이블카를 타고 올라가면 식당과 커피숍이 있는데 그곳에 유명한 서울타워(Seoul Tower)가 있다. 민지와 나는 엘리베이터를 타고 서울타워 위에 있는 식당에 가서 점심도 먹고 커피도 마셨다.

G6.2   The use of the plain style in speaking

(1) [마크 and 동수 are waiting for a bus. 마크 sees a bus coming.]
마크: 버스 온**다**!

(2) [마크 has been looking for a file, and he sees it.]
찾았**다**!

(3) [마크 wants to take 민지 hiking tomorrow.]
마크: 민지야, 너 내일 등산 갈 거**니**?
민지: 아니, 피곤해서 그냥 집에서 쉴까 해.
마크: 그러지 말고 같이 가**자**.
　　　　나 혼자 가면 재미없잖아.
민지: 그래, 좋아. 그럼 내일 아침에 전화할래?
마크: 알았어. 내일 보**자**. 시간 지**켜라**.

   Notes

1. Occasionally, with slight modification in forms, the plain style, rather than the intimate ~어/아 style, is used when speaking to a child listener, to an intimate friend, or to a sibling.

2. Unlike the polite style and the intimate style, which do not have separate endings for different sentence types, the plain style uses different endings for different sentence types:

~다:	statement
~느냐/(으)냐/니:[a]	question
~어라/아라:[b]	command, request
~자:	proposal

a. In writing, verbs take ~느냐 and adjectives take ~(으)냐. In speaking, however, ~냐 or ~니 is used regardless of whether it is a verb or an adjective.

b. The ~어라/아라 variation is due to the same vowel harmony rule as for the ~어(요)/아(요) and ~어서/아서 variation.

3. There are some contexts that particularly call for the use of the plain style in conversation. The statement-ending ~다, for example, is used when the speaker wants to draw the listener's attention because the information is noteworthy or provoking, as in (1) and (2). As in (3), the question-ending ~니, the proposal-ending ~자, and the command-ending ~라 give a sense of more personal attachment to the conveyed message than if the intimate ~어/아 style were used. With the question-ending ~니, for example, the speaker may show more of his/her curiosity or eagerness to know. The use of ~자 in making a proposal sounds more personal, affectionate, and appealing.

Notes

Exercises

1. Fill in the blank with the proper form of the plain style for the given verb.

(1)   A: 여기서는 택시 잡기 <u>힘드니</u> (힘들다)?

       B: 응. 큰 길로 <u>가 보자</u> (가 보다).

(2)   아버지: 민수 _____ (일어나다)?

       민지: 아직 안 일어났어요.

(3)   스티브: 나 숙제 좀 보여 줄래?

       민지: 공부 좀 _____ (하다)! 숙제는 혼자 해야지.

                  친구 거 빌리면 어떻게 _____ (하다)?

(4)   [스티브 is trying to figure out a puzzle. He finally finds the solution.]

       _____ (알다)!

(5)   스티브: 동수야, 너 내일 등산 _____ (가다)?

       동수: 숙제 할 것도 있고 해서 집에서 쉴까 하는데.

       스티브: 그러지 말고 같이 _____ (가다).

2. How would you say the following expressions in Korean? Choose an appropriate speech style (i.e., deferential, polite, intimate, or plain style) according to each context.

(1)   You are introducing yourself to an adult Korean speaker.

      "Glad to meet you." (*Lit.*, "I am meeting you for the first time.")

      "I'm _____(your name)."

(2)   You are talking to a child. "What's your name? How old are you?"

(3)   You are being interviewed by a reporter from a Korean television station. The reporter compliments your Korean language ability. How would you respond?

(4)   You are talking to a co-worker, "Let's go eat lunch."

(5)   You are asking a child, "Where is your father?"

(6)   You are calling your professor's office and say, "May I speak to Professor Kim please?"

G6.3 V.S.~기로 하다 'plan to/decide to'

(1) A: 이번 여름 방학에 뭐 하**기로 했어요**?   What did you decide to do this summer break?

B: 6월에 한국에 가**기로 했어요**.   I decided to go to Korea in June.

(2) 친구하고 등산 가**기로 했**는데 감기 때문에 못 갔어요.

(3) A: 생일에 뭐 하**기로 했어요**?

B: 저녁 먹고 나서 영화 보러 가**기로 했어요**.

(4) A: 이번 학기에 졸업하지요?

B: 아니요, 서두르지 않**기로 했어요**.

✦ Notes

1. The construction [V.S.~기로 하다] expresses a decision or determination.
2. The negative form is expressed by 안 + verb + 기로 하다 or verb + 지 않기로 하다.

> 컴퓨터 게임을 안 하기로 했어요. = 컴퓨터 게임을 하지 않기로 했어요.

Exercises

1. Give an appropriate response using ~기로 하다.

(1) A: 점심 먹었어요?

     B: 수잔 씨하고 두 시 반에 같이 <u>먹기로 했어요</u>.

(2) 주말에 뭐 하실 거예요?

    _____

(3) 수잔이랑 어디에서 만나기로 했어요?

    _____

(4) 크리스마스에 뭐 해요?

    _____

(5) 남자/여자 친구를 언제 또 만나요?

    _____

(6) 어머니날에 무슨 선물 살 거예요?

    _____

2. You are traveling with your friends. You came up with the following schedule. Compose a narrative using ~기로 하다.

겨울 방학 여행	
1월 5일 (일)	인천국제공항 오후 4시 출발
1월 5일 (일)	뉴욕 케네디 공항 밤 9시 도착 (맨해튼 호텔)
1월 6일 (월)	오후 6시 브로드웨이 쇼 (show)
1월 7일 (화)	나이아가라 폭포 (fall)
1월 8일 (수)	토론토 다운타운에서 쇼핑
1월 9일 (목)	케네디 공항 출발

3. Do you make New Year's resolutions? Say three things you decided to do and three things you decided not to do this year.

   (1) <u>올해는 매일 일기를 쓰기로 했어요</u>.

   (2) _____

   (3) _____

   (4) _____

   (5) <u>올해는 담배를 피우지 않기로 했어요</u>.

   (6) _____

   (7) _____

   (8) _____

Notes

Conversation 2 관악산 입구까지 가 주세요.

▌ 스티브가 지하철역에서 교통 카드 파는 곳을 찾고 있다.

Conversation 2

스티브:	저어, 실례지만, 말씀 좀 묻겠습니다.
여자:	네.
스티브:	여기 교통 카드는 어디서 사야 돼요?
여자:	지금 발매기는 좀 복잡하니까
	저기 편의점에서 사세요.
스티브:	네, 감사합니다.

▌ 스티브가 서울대입구역에서
내려서 택시를 잡으려고 손을 흔든다.

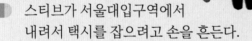

기사:	손님, 어디까지 가세요?
스티브:	관악산 입구요.
기사:	네, 알겠습니다.
스티브:	길이 많이 막히네요.
기사:	등산객이 많아서 그래요. 라디오에서 이번 주에
	단풍이 제일 아름답다고 하네요.[G6.4]
스티브:	아, 그래요? 제가 운이 좋은 것 같네요. 그런데
	기사님, 10시까지 가야 되는데 괜찮을까요?
기사:	아무리 서둘러도[G6.5] 10시까지는 힘들겠는데요.
	스트레스도 풀 수 있어서 좋아요.

COMPREHENSION QUESTIONS

1. 스티브는 표를 어디서 사야 합니까?
2. 스티브는 지하철을 타고 어디까지 갑니까?
3. 관악산 입구까지 어떻게 갑니까?
4. 스티브는 몇 시까지 관악산 입구에 가야 합니까?
5. 관악산 가는 길이 왜 막힙니까?

NEW WORDS

NOUN

경찰	police
고속도로	highway, freeway
공사	construction
교통카드	transportation card
등산객	mountain climber
마을 버스	town shuttle bus
발매기	vending machine
사고	accident
술	alcoholic beverage
운	luck, fortune
인도	sidewalk
장소	place, location
차도	street, road
편의점	convenience store
(교통) 표지판	(traffic) sign
환승(하다)	transfer
횡단보도	crosswalk

VERB

(사고) 나다	to happen, occur
늘다	to improve
모이다	to gather
이용하다	to utilize

ADJECTIVE

외롭다	to be lonely

SUFFIX

~다/라/자/냐고 하다	say that
아무리 ~어/아도	no matter how

NEW EXPRESSIONS

In 제가 운이 좋은 것 같아요, the expression 운이 좋다 [*lit.*, 'the luck is good'.] means 'be lucky, fortunate; to have good luck'. The noun 운 'luck' can be used in the following ways:

저는 운이 좋아요.	I have good luck.
제가 운이 있어요.	I have luck; I am lucky.
철수는 운이 별로 안 좋아요.	Cheolsu doesn't have good luck.
올해는 제가 운이 나빠요.	This year, I have bad luck.

Grammar

G6.4   Indirect quotation: ~다고 하다, ~(으/느)냐고 하다, ~(으)라고 하다, ~자고 하다

Statement: ~(는/ㄴ)다고 하다/~(이)라고 하다

(1) 마크: 여보세요. 동수 좀 부탁합니다.

  누나: 동수 아직 안 들어왔는데요.   동수 hasn't come home yet.
      오늘 좀 늦는**다고 했어요**.   *He said that* he would be
              a little late today.

  마크: 저 마크인데요, 동수
      들어오면 제가 전화했**다고**
      전해 주세요.

(2) 요즘 공사 때문에 길이 막힌**다고 한다**.

(3) 제임스는 대학원생**이라고 했어요**.

Request: ~(으)라고 하다/~지 말라고 하다

(4) 고속도로에서 운전할 때는 표지판을 잘 보**라고 한다**.

(5) 선생님이 수업에 늦지 말**라고 하셨다**.

(6) 경찰이 차도 말고 횡단보도를 이용하**라고 했다**.

Proposal: ~자고 하다

(7) 동수가 친구들에게 한국 음식을 먹**자고 했다**.

(8) 동수가 영미한테 여행을 가**자고 했다**.

Question: ~(으/느)냐고 하다/묻다

(9) 동수가 나한테 언제 미국에 가**냐고 했다**.

(10) 직원한테 어디서 기차를 타**느냐고 물었다**.

Notes

1. Indirect quotation is used when the speaker quotes what somebody else said or when the speaker passes his/her or someone else's thought to the listener. It takes the various forms of [QUOTED MESSAGE]고 하다.

 (i)   . . . 고 해/해요/한다/합니다 when quoting a general
       message that is currently going around
 (ii) . . . 고 했어/했어요/했다/했습니다 when quoting a specific
       message that was said in the past
 (iii) . . . 고 하셔/하세요/하신다/하십니다 in the present tense,
       . . . 고 하셨어/하셨어요/하셨다/하셨습니다 in the past
       tense when the quoted message is/was said by someone
       who is respected (i.e., the honorific forms of 하다 are used)
 (iv) In colloquial speech, especially in Seoul, the indirect
       quotation takes the verb 그래(요)/그랬어(요) instead
       of 해요/했어(요). Also, the quotation particle 고 is often
       deleted in colloquial speech. For example,

 마크: 여보세요, 동수 좀 바꿔 주세요.
 동수 누나: 동수 아직 안 들어 왔는데요.
                오늘 좀 늦는다(고) 그랬어요.

2. The quoted message itself also takes different endings of the plain style depending on the sentence type of the quoted message,—that is, whether it is a statement, question, command, or proposal,—and on the time of the event in the quoted message.

 (i)   ~(는/ㄴ/었)다고 하다 when the quoted message is a statement
       V~는다고 하다 with a verb whose stem ends in a consonant
       V~ㄴ다고 하다 with a verb stem ending in a vowel
       A~다고 하다 with an adjective
       ~라고 하다 with the copula ~이
       V/A~었/았다고 하다 when the event in the quoted
       message occurred prior to the actual saying of the message.

(ii) ~느냐/(으)냐/었느냐고 하다 when the quoted message is a question
    V~느냐고 하다 with a verb
    A~(으)냐고 하다 with an adjective and the copula
    V/A~었았/느냐고 하다

(iii) ~(으)라고 하다 when the quoted message is a command or request.
    Note that ~(으)라 is used instead of ~어라/아라 of the plain style.

(iv) ~자고 하다 when the quoted message is a proposal.

	Standard	Colloquial
Statement		
	V~는/ㄴ다고 해(요)/했어(요)	~는/ㄴ다(고) 그래(요)/그랬어(요)
	A~다고 해(요)/했어(요)	~다(고) 그래(요)/그랬어(요)
	~었다고 해(요)/했어(요)	~었다고 그래(요)/그랬어(요)
Question		
	V~느냐고 해(요)/했어(요)	~느냐 그래(요))/그랬어(요)
	A~(으)냐고 해(요)/했어(요)	~(으)냐 그래(요))/그랬어(요)
	~었/았느냐고 해(요)/했어(요)	~었/았느냐 그래(요))/그랬어(요)
Command/Request/Proposal		
	V~(으)라고 해(요)/했어(요)	~(으)라 그래(요)/그랬어(요)
	V~자고 해(요)/했어(요)	~자 그래(요)/그랬어(요)

3. The act of saying may be indicated by a different verb than 하다 if the specific nature of saying is to be specified, as in (1) and (10):

~다/라고 전해 주다   Convey/pass along the message that . . .
~느냐/(으)냐고 물어보다   Ask if/whether . . .

Sample conjugations of indirect discourse

			Present tense	Past tense
V e r b s	Statement	**먹다**	먹는다고 했어요/그랬어요	먹었다고 했어요/그랬어요
	Question		먹느냐고 했어요/그랬어요	먹었느냐고 했어요/그랬어요
	Command		먹으라고 했어요/그랬어요	
	Proposal		먹자고 했어요/그랬어요	
	Statement	**사다**	산다고 했어요/그랬어요	샀다고 했어요/그랬어요
	Question		사느냐고 했어요/그랬어요	샀느냐고 했어요/그랬어요
	Command		사라고 했어요/그랬어요	
	Proposal		사자고 했어요/그랬어요	
A d j e c t i v e s	Statement	**좋다**	좋다고 했어요/그랬어요	좋았다고 했어요/그랬어요
	Question		좋으냐고 했어요/그랬어요	좋았느냐고 했어요/그랬어요
	Statement	**예쁘다**	예쁘다고 했어요/그랬어요	예뻤다고 했어요/그랬어요
	Question		예쁘냐고 했어요/그랬어요	예뻤느냐고 했어요/그랬어요

4. The indirect quotation ~다고 해요/그래요 is similar to the hearsay expression ~대(요)/래(요) in that the speaker conveys somebody else's message or thought. The difference between the two is that the main purpose of the hearsay expression ~대(요)/래(요), as in 스티브가 자고 있대요, is to convey the content of the message itself, often even without revealing who the primary speaker is, whereas the main purpose of the indirect quotation ~다고 해요/그래요 is to quote someone's speech.

Exercise

1. Using the indirect quotation form, make up an utterance according to the given context.

(1)　[동수:　　　누나, 나 오늘 좀 늦을 거야.]
　　　스티브:　　여보세요, 동수 좀 부탁합니다.
　　　동수누나:　동수 아직 안 들어 왔는데요.
　　　　　　　　<u>오늘 좀 늦는다고 했어요</u>.

(2)　[민지:　　　스티브, 나 수업 끝날 때까지 기다려.]
　　　동수:　　　스티브, 빨리 가자.
　　　스티브:　　먼저 가. 나 민지 기다려야 돼.
　　　　　　　　_____

(3)　[스티브:　　오늘 차 사고가 나서 학교에 못 가요.]
　　　동수:　　　누나, 나한테 전화온 데 없어요?
　　　동수 누나:　스티브한테서 전화 왔는데,
　　　　　　　　_____

(4)　[스티브:　　누나, 동수 내일 몇 시에 학교에 가요?
　　　동수 누나:　잘 모르겠는데.]
　　　동수:　　　누나, 혹시 스티브가 전화 안 했어요?
　　　동수 누나:　응, 아까 스티브한테서 전화 왔는데,
　　　　　　　　내일 _____

(5)　[우진:　　　저 미국에서 온 우진이라고 하는데요.
　　　　　　　　동수 좀 바꿔 주세요]
　　　누나:　　　동수야, 전화 받어.
　　　　　　　　_____

(6)　[민지:　　　스티브, 내일 등산 나하고 같이 가.]
　　　동수:　　　민지도 내일 등산 같이 가니?
　　　스티브:　　응, 어제 전화 왔는데,
　　　　　　　　_____

2. Change into an indirect quotation.

(1) "자전거는 인도 말고 차도에서 타세요."
     <u>자전거는 인도 말고 차도에서 타라고 했습니다.</u>

(2) "밖에서 잠깐만 기다리세요."
     _____

(3) "방금 라디오에서 뉴스 들었어요?"
     _____

(4) "술 마시고 운전하지 마세요."
     _____

(5) "날씨도 좋은데 운동하러 공원에 갑시다."
     _____

(6) "이번 토요일에 다 같이 모이자."
     _____

(7) "수업 시간에 졸지 말고 공부하세요."
     _____

(8) "비가 오니까 우산 가지고 가세요."
     _____

3. Complete the following dialogues using the indirect quotation form ~고 하다.

(1) A: 왜 택시 안 타고 지하철을 타세요?
     B: 동수가 토요일은 길이 복잡하니까 <u>지하철 타라고 했어요.</u>

(2) A: 이번 토요일에 같이 등산 갈래요?
     B: 일기예보에서 이번 토요일에 _____
     A: 그래요? 그럼 안 되겠네요.

(3) A: 민지 씨 왜 안 와요?
     B: 아침에 중요한 약속이 있어서 늦게 _____

(4) A: 마크 씨가 한국에 온 지 1년이나 됐어요.
     B: 그래요? 나한테는 6개월밖에 _____

(5) A: 동수 씨 어제 민지 생일파티에 갔어요?
     B: 아마 갔을 거예요. 어제 집에 가다가 만났는데
     _____

G6.5   아무리 ~어도/아도 'no matter how . . .'

(1) 지하철역에서 내려서 도봉산
가는 마을버스를 기다리는데,
아무리 기다려도 오지 않아서
택시를 탔다.

I got off at the subway station and then waited for a town shuttle bus going to Dobong Mountain. Although I waited a long time, the bus didn't come, so I took a taxi.

(2) [민지 and 동수 are looking up a word in a dictionary.]
민지: 동수 씨, 아직도 못 찾았어요?
동수: 네, **아무리 찾아도** 못 찾겠어요.
민지씨가 한 번 찾아 봐요.

(3) 동수: 민지 씨, 스티브한테 연락했어요?
민지: **아무리 전화해도** 안 받는데요.

(4) 동수: 스티브 씨, 파티에 올 거예요?
스티브: 글쎄요. **아무리 생각해 봐도** 못 갈 것 같아요.

Notes

1. 아무리 ~어도/아도 is used when the intended goal could not be obtained even after maximum effort has been made. Hence, it is typically (but not always) followed by a negative expression indicating the failure to obtain the intended goal or effect.

2. The ~어도/아도 variation is the same as that of ~어요/아요, ~어서/아서, ~었/았-, etc.

Exercise

Using 아무리 ~어도/아도, make up a dialogue according to the given context.

(1) 민지: 여기 음식 참 많이 주지요?

동수: 네. <u>아무리 먹어도</u> 끝이 안 나네요.

(2) 민지: 스티브 씨, 날씨가 추운데 등산가실 거예요?

스티브: 네, _____ 등산 갈 거예요.

(3) 소연: 스티브 씨, 왜 그렇게 많이 먹어요?

스티브: 네, 하루 종일 식사를 못 해서요,

_____ 배가 고파요.

(4) 민지: 어제 동수 씨 오래 기다렸어요?

스티브: 네, 약속 장소에서 _____ 오지 않아서

그냥 집에 갔어요.

(5) 동수: 아니, 민지 씨, 스티브 씨하고 같이 오기로 하지 않았어요?

민지: 네. 근데 스티브 씨한테 _____

안 받아서 그냥 혼자 왔어요.

(6) 아무리 친구가 _____ 외로워요.

(7) A: 한국어를 정말 잘하시네요.

B: 아니에요. 아무리 _____ 한국어가 안 늘어요.

| Narration | 스티브의 일기 1 |

오늘은 아주 맑은 가을 날씨였다. 그래서 동수와 관악산으로 등산을 갔다 왔다. 관악산에 가려면 우리 학교 앞에서 서울대입구역까지 먼저 지하철을 타고 간 다음 버스로 갈아타야 한다. 서울에서는 교통 카드를 사용하면 지하철과 버스를 무료로 환승[1]할 수 있다. 그래서 어제 교통 카드를 처음 사 봤다. 발매기 앞에 줄[2]이 너무 길어서 편의점에서 샀다. 지하철을 타고 서울대입구역에서 내렸는데 길이 복잡해서 관악산으로 가는 버스 정류장을 못 찾았다. 그래서 택시를 탔는데 길이 많이 막혀서 약속 장소에 20분 늦게 도착했다. 약속 시간을 못 지켜서 동수에게 미안했다. 그렇지만 오래간만에 복잡한 도시를 떠나서 자연[3]을 즐길[4] 수 있어서 좋았다.

1. 환승(하다): transfer
2. 줄: line
3. 자연: nature
4. 즐기다: to enjoy

COMPREHENSION QUESTIONS

1. 어느 계절입니까?
2. 관악산에는 어떻게 갑니까?
3. 스티브는 왜 승차권을 샀습니까?
4. 스티브는 어디서 표를 샀습니까?
5. 스티브는 왜 늦었습니까?

Notes

CULTURE

주민등록증

미국에는 사회보장번호(Social Security number)가 있고 한국에는 주민등록번호(Resident Registration number)가 있다. 주민등록번호는 모두 13자리의 숫자[1]로 되어 있는데,  앞의 여섯 자리는 생년월일[2]을 나타낸다[3]. 예를 들어[4] 1995년 8월 24일 생의 주민등록 번호 앞자리는 950824가 된다. 뒤의 일곱자리 중 첫 자리[5]는 성별[6]을 나타낸다. 남자는 1 (950824-1XXXXXX) 혹은 3, 여자는 2 혹은 4가 된다(950824-2XXXXXX). 그래서 주민등록번호를 보면 그 사람의 나이와 성별을 쉽게 알 수 있다. 모든 사람들의 주민등록 번호가 다르기 때문에,

주민등록번호는 본인 확인[7]이 필요할 경우 많이 쓰인다[8]. 신용카드나 은행 계좌를 만들 때 그리고 새로 핸드폰을 사서 쓸 때도 주민등록번호가 필요하다. 한국에서 오래 사는 외국인들의 경우에는 외국인등록번호(Alien Registration number)를 받게 된다.

1. 숫자: number
2. 생년월일: date of birth
3. 나타내다: to show, represent
4. 예를 들어: for example
5. 자리: digit
6. 성별: sex
7. 본인 확인: self-identification
8. 쓰이다: to be used

USAGE

1 Asking for and giving directions

(1) A: 저어, 실례지만, 말씀 좀 묻겠습니다.
      여기 표 사는 곳이 어디 있어요?
   B: 어디까지 가세요?
   A: "관악역"이요.
   B: 외국분 같은데 제가 도와 드릴게요. 이쪽으로 오세요.
   A: 감사합니다.
   B: 뭘요.

(2) A: 저어, 실례합니다.
   B: 네.
   A: 시청까지 바로 가는 버스 있어요?
   B: 바로 가는 건 없고 18번을 타고 가다가
      6번으로 갈아타야 돼요.
   A: 감사합니다.

When you ask for directions on the street, you can start by saying something like "저어, 실례합니다. 말씀 좀 묻겠습니다." (저어, as a conversation opener, expresses hesitation.)

Exercise 1

Converse with your partner on the following topics.

(1) 지금 어디 사세요?
(2) 주소가 어떻게 돼요?
(3) 학교에서 어떻게 가는지 약도 좀 그려 주실래요?

Exercise 2

You are invited to your friend's house for Thanksgiving dinner. You need to get directions to your friend's place. Take the roles of both parties.

 **Exercise 3**

Your Korean teacher invites you to a barbecue. Call the teacher to get the directions to his/her place from the classroom and draw a map. Then compare your map with that of others.

Useful words for city guide (도시 안내)

시청 (city hall)	경찰서 (a police station)
소방서 (a fire station)	박물관 (a museum)
모텔/호텔 (an inn/hotel)	공장 (a factory)
상점/가게 (a store)	제과점/빵집 (a bakery)
노래방 (a karaoke room)	술집 (a pub, a bar)
세탁소 (a laundry)	이발소 (a barbershop)
미용실 (a beauty salon)	동물원 (a zoo)
고층빌딩 (a high-rise building)	간판 (store signs)
차도 (a road for vehicles)	인도 (a sidewalk)
신호등 (a traffic signal)	시내 (downtown)
네거리/사거리 (intersection)	주유소 (a gas station)
버스 정류장 (a bus stop)	지하철 입구 (a subway entrance)
상가 (the business section)	지하 상가 (an underground market)
방송국 (a broadcasting station)	신문사 (a newspaper publisher)

Notes

. . . .

. . . .

. . . .

. . . .

. . . .

. . . .

2　*Using public transportation*

(1)　(택시 타기)
　　기사:　손님, 어디로 모실까요?
　　마크:　도봉산 입구까지 가 주세요.

(2)　(택시 안에서)
　　기사:　도봉산 입구에 거의 다 왔는데, 어디 세워 드릴까요?
　　마크:　저기 신호등 지나서 지하도 입구에서 세워 주세요.
　　기사:　알겠습니다.
　　마크:　(택시 미터기를 보면서) 여기 2,500원 있습니다.
　　기사:　감사합니다. 안녕히 가세요.

(3)　(기차역에서)
　　A:　　서울-부산 왕복 하나 주세요.
　　B:　　창가 자리로 드릴까요, 복도 쪽으로 드릴까요?
　　A:　　창가 쪽으로 주세요. 얼마예요?
　　B:　　만오천 원입니다.
　　(기차역 train station, 창가 자리 a window seat, 복도 an aisle seat)

Expressions that you hear from a taxi driver:

　　어디까지 가세요? / 어디로 모실까요?
　　어디 세워 드릴까요?

Telling the destination:

　　＿＿＿＿＿＿＿(destination)에 가 주세요.
　　＿＿＿＿＿＿＿(destination)~(이)요.
　　＿＿＿＿＿＿＿(location)에 세워 주세요.

Asking for the taxi fare:

　　얼마예요?
　　얼마 나왔어요?
　　얼마 드리면 돼요?

Making a request:

　　아저씨, 시간이 없으니까 좀 더 빨리 가 주세요.
　　위험하니까 천천히 가 주세요.

Exercise 1

Suppose you are learning Korean in 서울. You want to visit 경주 by train next Saturday. You need a round-trip train ticket from 서울 to 경주. Take the roles of the customer and a clerk at a ticket counter.

3　*Making telephone calls*

Examples

(1) Taking and leaving a message

영미:	여보세요, 우진이 집에 있어요?
우진 형:	없는데요. 오늘 좀 늦는다고 했어요.
영미:	저, 우진이 친구 영미라고 하는데요.
	우진이 들어오면 영미가 전화했다고 좀 전해 주세요.
우진 형:	네, 그러죠.
영미:	고맙습니다. 안녕히 계세요.

(2) Returning a telephone call

우진:	영미, 나야, 아까 전화했다면서? 무슨 일이야?
영미:	응, 숙제를 하다가 모르는 게 있어서 전화했는데,
	내일 학교에서 좀 만날 수 있어?
우진:	그래. 몇 시에 만날까?
영미:	아침 10시 도서관 앞에서 어때?
우진:	응, 좋아. 마침 나도 그 때 수업이 없으니까 잘 됐네.
영미:	고마워, 그럼 내일 도서관 앞에서 만나.
우진:	응, 그래. 끊어.

(3) Wrong numbers

A:	여보세요.
B:	여보세요. 최성호 씨 좀 부탁합니다.
A:	여기 그런 사람 없는데요. 몇 번에 거셨어요?
B:	거기 567-7890 아니에요?
A:	아닌데요. 전화 잘못 거셨어요. 여긴 7895예요.
B:	죄송합니다.

Useful expressions

통화 중이에요.	The line is busy.
전화 잘못 거셨어요.	You have the wrong number.
지역 번호가 뭐예요?	What is the area code?
자동 응답기에 메시지를	Please leave a message on the
남겨 주세요.	answering machine.
전화가 고장 났어요.	The phone is out of order.
잠깐만 기다리세요./잠깐만요.	Hold on please.
전화기	the telephone (machine) set
장거리 전화	a long-distance call
전화 회사	a telephone company
국제 전화	an international call
전화비	a telephone bill
전화를 걸다/끊다	to call/to hang up

Exercise 1

Converse with your partner about the following questions.

(1) 한국말로 전화해 본 적이 있으세요?

(2) 전화기를 혼자 쓰세요? 아니면 다른 사람이랑 같이 쓰세요?

(3) 집에 전화기가 몇 대 있으세요? 어디 어디 있어요?

(4) 누구한테 전화를 제일 자주 하세요? 얼마나 자주 전화하세요?

(5) 전화하는 걸 좋아하세요?

(6) 어느 장거리 전화 회사를 사용하세요? 왜요?

(7) 한 달에 전화비가 얼마나 나와요?

Exercise 2

Practice the following telephone conversation.

영미: 여보세요, 저 우진이 친구 영미라고 하는데요.
우진이 있으면 좀 부탁합니다.

우진 형: 아직 학교에서 안 돌아왔는데요.

영미: 우진이 들어오면 <u>영미가 전화했다고</u>
좀 전해 주시겠어요?

우진 형: 네, 그러죠.

영미: 고맙습니다. 안녕히 계세요.

Practice the above conversation again, substituting the underlined part with the following messages.

(1) 영미 is in the library now.

(2) 영미 is waiting for 우진 in front of the library.

(3) 영미 already went home.

(4) 영미 called to invite 우진 to her birthday party.

(5) 영미 called to ask when the Korean test will take place.

Exercise 3

Someone just dialed your number by mistake. Make a dialogue.

Exercise 4

With your classmate, make a telephone dialogue using the intimate speech style for the following situations.

(1) You missed Korean class today because you had a cold.
You call your classmate James to find out about any
assignment due. James says that there is no homework for
tomorrow, but there will be a quiz on lesson 5 tomorrow.

(2) You have to go to the airport tomorrow morning to pick up
your parents. You are going to miss Korean class.
You ask your classmate to tell your Korean teacher that
you will turn in your homework the day after tomorrow.

Exercise 5

You call to talk with 영미. She is not home. Leave a voice message for her to call you back; give the time and your phone number.

Exercise 6

Your younger sister's friend (수미) calls to speak with your sister (영희). She is not home. Take a message.

| 4 | *Writing a journal* |

10월 20일 토요일 (날씨: 아주 맑음)

오늘은 아주 화창한 가을 날씨였다. 시험이 끝나서 같은 반 친구들이
도봉산으로 등산을 가자고 했다. 전에 도봉산 쪽으로 가 본 적이 없어서
동수한테 교통편을 물어 보았다. 동수는 나한테 지하철을 타고 도봉역까지
가서 거기서부터는 도봉산 행 버스를 타라고 가르쳐 주었다.

나는 동수 말대로 가까운 지하철역으로 내려가서 어느 아주머니의
도움으로 자동 발매기에서 표를 산 다음 도봉역에서 내렸다. 그런데
아무리 기다려도 도봉산으로 가는 버스가 오지 않았다. 약속 시간에 늦을
것 같아서 택시를 탔는데 다행히 약속 시간에 맞추어 도착했다. 오래간만에
복잡한 도시를 떠나서 친구들과 마음껏 하루를 즐길 수 있었다.

Example

The plain speech style is usually used in journals.

Exercise 1

Write a journal entry about your past weekend using the plain speech style. (Challenge: Read your journal to the class.)

Lesson 6 Public Transportation

CONVERSATION 1 *Are you all prepared for hiking?*

Dongsoo makes a call to Steve's cell phone.

Dongsoo:	Oh, Steve, I'm sorry. I couldn't answer the phone before because the battery had run out.
Steve:	Oh, that's all right. I called because we decided to go hiking to Gwanak Mountain this weekend, you know. But Woojin is not likely to go since an important thing suddenly came up for this weekend.
Dongsoo:	Is that so? It's too bad. It would be nice if he could go as well. But we cannot help it. Are you all prepared to hike?
Steve:	Yes. By the way, is there a bus that goes directly from the front of the school to Gwanak Mountain?
Dongsoo:	No bus goes directly; you have to transfer on the way. First take a subway to the Seoul University Station; there, transfer to a bus.
Steve:	I got it. I'll see you this Saturday morning at the entrance to Gwanak Mountain.

CONVERSATION 2 *Please go to the entrance to Gwanak Mountain.*

Steve is looking for a place to buy a ticket at the subway station.

Steve:	Excuse me, may I ask a question? Where is the place that sells tickets here?
Woman:	Buy a ticket from the vending machine over there because the ticket office is crowded now.
Steve:	Okay, thank you.

Steve gets off at the Seoul University Station and waves his hand to catch a taxi.

Driver:	Sir, where are you going?
Steve:	To the entrance to Gwanak Mountain.
Driver:	Okay, I got it.
Steve:	The road is really congested.
Driver:	That is because there are many mountain hikers. People say that the autumn foliage is the most beautiful this week.
Steve:	Oh, is that so? I think I am lucky.
Driver:	By what time should you get there?
Steve:	By 10 o'clock.
Driver:	No matter how much we hurry, it will be hard to get there by 10 o'clock.

| NARRATION | *Steve's diary* |

October 30, Saturday

Today the autumn weather was very clear, so I went hiking up Gwanak Mountain with Dongsoo. To go to Gwanak Mountain, one has to take a subway in front of the school to the Seoul University Station and transfer to a bus. In Seoul, it is free to transfer from a subway to a bus if you use a transportation card. However, since I lost my transportation card yesterday, I just bought a ticket. The ticket office was crowded, so I bought a ticket from a vending machine with the help of a lady. I took a subway and got off at the Seoul University Station, but I couldn't find the bus stop to Gwanak Mountain because the roads were complicated. Thus, I took a taxi, but I arrived at the appointed place ten minutes late because the road was really congested. I felt sorry for Dongsoo because I didn't meet him at the appointed time. It was nice to leave the crowded city after a long while and enjoy nature.

| CULTURE | 주민등록증 |

The Resident Registration number in Korea is similar to the Social Security number in America. The Resident Registration number is composed of thirteen digits, of which the first six represent the person's birthday. For example, the first six digits for someone who was born on August 24, 1995, are 950824. The first digit of the other seven digits represents gender: 1 or 3 for male and 2 or 4 for female. Therefore, you can figure out a person's age and gender easily by just looking at the Resident Registration number. Since everybody's number is unique, the number is often used when identification is needed. You need the Resident Registration number when you get credit cards or open bank accounts and when you want to buy a new cell phone and start the phone service. Foreigners who live in Korea for a long time receive an Alien Registration number.

7과 가게에서

Lesson 7 At a Store

Conversation 1　　사과 한 상자에 얼마예요?

▶ 우진이는 과일을 사러 동네 과일 가게에 갔다.

Conversation　1

우진:　안녕하세요, 아주머니.

주인:　어, 학생, 오래간만이에요.

우진:　네, 방학 동안 어디 좀 갔다 왔어요.

주인:　그랬어요?

우진:　와, 과일이 맛있어 보이네요.^{G7.1}

　　　요즘 어떤 과일이 잘 팔려요?^{G7.2}

주인:　사과하고 배가 잘 팔리는 편이에요.

우진:　사과는 한 상자에 얼마예요?

주인:　삼만 원이에요.

우진:　한 상자에 몇 개나 들어 있어요?^{G7.3}

주인:　열 개 들어 있어요.

우진:　이 귤도 맛있겠네요. 귤은 얼마예요?

주인:　열 개에 오천 원이에요.

우진:　그럼 귤 만 원어치만 주세요.

COMPREHENSION QUESTIONS

1. 우진이는 방학에 무엇을 했습니까?
2. 요즘은 어떤 과일이 잘 팔립니까?
3. 우진이는 사과 한 상자에 얼마입니까?
4. 우진이는 귤을 얼마어치 샀습니까?

NEW WORDS

NOUN

과일	fruit
귤	tangerine
도둑	thief
두부	tofu
배	pear
사과	apple
생선	fish
소리	sound, noise
약	medicine
우체부	postman

PRONOUN

누가	someone
뭐	something
어디	somewhere
언제	sometime

VERB

깎다	to cut down
닫히다	to be closed
물다	to bite
물리다	to be bitten
뺏기다	to be deprived of
열리다	to be open
잡히다	to be caught
팔리다	to be sold

ADJECTIVE

행복하다	to be happy

SUFFIX

어치	worth, value
~어/아 보이다	to appear, look
~어/아 있다	to be in the state of

NEW EXPRESSIONS

1. The question words 뭐, 누구, 어디, and 언제 are also used as indefinite pronouns. Indefinite pronouns are used when the speaker has no specific referent in mind such as someone/anyone, something/anything, somewhere/anywhere, some/any time, etc. in English.

2. 어치 'worth' is a suffix that attaches to an amount. Following are some

천 원어치	an amount that is worth 1,000 won
얼마어치	how much (in money)

사과 얼마어치 드릴까요?	How much worth of apples do you want?
오천 원어치만 주세요.	Just give me 5,000 won's worth.

Grammar

G7.1   ~어/아 보이다 'someone/something appears . . . , looks . . .'

(1) 스티브: 민지 씨, 헤어스타일이 바뀌었네요.
             민지 씨 얼굴하고 잘 어울리는데요.
      민지: 네, 스티브 씨도 머리 깎으니까 시원**해 보여요**.

(2) 스시가 맛있**어 보여요**. The sushi looks delicious.

(3) 구두가 멋있**어 보여요**. Those shoes look cool.

(4) 제인: 이 생선 어때요?
             괜찮**아 보여요**?
      제프: 네, 싱싱**해 보이**는데요.

(5) A: 오랜만이에요.
      B: 네, 바**빠 보이**시네요. 언제 저녁 같이 먹어요. .
             You look busy. We should have dinner sometime.
      A: 네, 그래요.

(6) 자동차가 비**싸 보여요**.

Examples

Notes

1. ~어/아 보이다 is used when commenting about the surface appearance of something; the speaker does not claim that the statement is factual.

2. ~어/아 보이다 is attached only to adjectives.

Citation form	Gloss	~어/아요	~어/아 보여요
시원하다	to be refreshing, cool	시원해요	시원해 보여요
싱싱하다	to be fresh	싱싱해요	싱싱해 보여요
무겁다	to be heavy	무거워요	무거워 보여요
맛있다	to be tasty	맛있어요	맛있어 보여요
멋있다	to be fancy, stylish, cool	멋있어요	멋있어 보여요
비싸다	to be expensive	비싸요	비싸 보여요

Notes

Exercises

1. Choosing from the given vocabulary, give a statement of appearance based on the given cue.

> 행복하다, 건강하다, 기분이 좋다, 기분이 나쁘다, 춥다, 시원하다

(1) [스티브가 머리를 깎았어요.] 시원해 보여요.

(2) [동수가 지갑을 잃어버렸어요.] _____

(3) [민지는 운동히 열심히 했어요.] _____

(4) [스티브는 입술이 파래요.] _____

(5) [제니는 지난 주에 결혼했어요.] _____

G7.2   Passive verbs

(1) 우진: 요즘 어떤 옷이 유행이에요?
    점원: 요즘은 밝은 색 옷이 잘 **팔려**요.

(2) 기사: 어디 세워 드릴까요?
    스티브: 저기 신호등 **보이**지요? 저 신호등 지나서 세워 주세요.

(3) 동생한테 좋아하는 시계를 **뺏겼**어요.
    I had my favorite watch taken away by my younger sister.

(4) A: 무슨 소리가 났는데 못 들었어요?
         I heard a sound. Didn't you hear it?

    B: 바람에 문이 **닫히**는 소리예요.
         It's the sound of the door being closed by the wind.

(5) 도둑이 경찰한테 **잡혔**다. The thief was caught by the police.

Examples

Notes

1. A situation is typically described from the point of view of the actor of an action. A situation may occasionally be described, however, from the point of view of the object of an action.

In English, passive forms are used for that purpose (e.g., The door is being opened/closed. The thief was caught by the police yesterday.) The passive construction in English is made grammatically by using the copula 'be' along with the past participle form of the verb (e.g., to be opened). In Korean, the passive construction is made with the suffix ~이, ~히, ~리, or ~기 attached to a verb stem, creating a new word.

개가 우체부를 물었어요 (물다).
A dog bit the postman.

우체부가 개한테 물렸어요 (물+리+다 → 물리다).
The postman was bitten by a dog.

2. Passives are used more often in English than in Korean. In English, almost all transitive verbs can be made into passives. In Korean, however, only a limited number of transitive verbs can be made passive.

3. Which verb is subject to this passive verb formation, as well as which verb takes which suffix among ~이, ~히, ~리, and ~기, simply has to be learned. We will classify them by the suffix a verb stem takes.

(i) ~이 types		
Active	**Passive**	**Example**
보다 to see (신호등을 못 봤어요.)	보이다	저기 신호등(이) 보이지요? Can you see the traffic light over there?
쓰다 to use (이 꽃 결혼식에 쓸 거예요?)	쓰이다	이 꽃은 결혼식에 잘 쓰여요. This flower is often used for weddings.

(ii) ~히 types

Active	Passive	Example
닫다 to close (문 좀 닫아 주세요.)	닫히다	바람에 문이 닫혔어요. The door was closed by the wind.
막다 to block (경찰이 길을 막았어요.)	막히다	차가 너무 많아서 길이 막혔어요. Because there were too many cars, traffic was blocked.
잡다 to catch (경찰이 도둑을 잡았어요)	잡히다	도둑이 경찰한테 잡혔어요. The thief was caught by the police.

(iii) ~리 types

Active	Passive	Example
물다 to bite (개가 우체부 다리를 물었어요.)	물리다	우체부는 개한테 다리를 물렸어요. The mail carrier was bitten by a dog on his/her leg.
열다 to open (이 가게 언제 열어요?)	열리다	가게가 열렸어요. The store has been opened.
듣다 to hear (라디오 자주 들으세요?)	들리다	우리 라디오가 잘 안 들려요. Our radio cannot be heard.
팔다 to sell (요새 집 많이 파세요?)	팔리다	요새는 집이 잘 안 팔려요. These days houses are not sold often.

(iv) ~기 types

Active	Passive	Example
뺏다 to take away from (오빠가 동생 사과를 뺏었어요.)	뺏기다	오빠한테 사과를 뺏겼어요. She had her apple taken away by her brother.
안다 to hold, hug (엄마가 아이를 안았습니다)	안기다	아이가 엄마한테 안겼습니다. The baby was held by Mom.
쫓다 to chase (개가 고양이를 쫓습니다.)	쫓기다	고양이가 개한테 쫓기고 있습니다. The cat is being chased by the dog.

4. With active verbs, actors are marked, if necessary, with the subject particle 이/가 or the topic particle 은/는, whereas the objects are marked with the object particle 을/를. With passive verbs, it is the objects that are marked with either the subject particle 이/가 or the topic particle 은/는, and the actors or instigators are marked, if necessary, with the dative particle 한테 if animate, 에 if inanimate.

Exercises

Fill in the blank with the appropriate form of a verb, active or passive. Choose the proper verb from the given list, based on the given context.

팔다   열다   닫다   보다   듣다   뺏다

(1) 우진: 요즘 어떤 옷이 유행이에요?

점원: 요즘은 밝은 색 옷이 잘 <u>팔려</u>요.

(2) A: 어디서 좋은 클래식 음악이 <u>들리</u>는데요.

B: 클래식 음악 자주 <u>들</u>_____?

A: 네, 자주 들어요.

(3) A: 무슨 소리예요?

B: 문이 바람에 _____ 소리예요.

(4) A: 동수가 안 _____. 어디 갔어요?

B: 가게에 두부 사러 나갔어요.

(5) A: 이 가방 좋은데요. 어디서 샀어요?

B: 산 게 아니고 언니한테 _____.

A: 언니가 동생한테 가방을 _____?

G7.3   ~어/아 있다 'In the state of being . . .'

(1) 손님: 이 사과 얼마해요?

주인: 한 상자에 10,000원이에요.

손님: 한 상자에 몇 개나 들**어 있어요**?   About how many are
                                                       in a box?

주인: 스무 개 들**어 있어요**.   Twenty are in (there).

(2) 지연: 어휴, 배 아파. 소연아, 약 있니?

소연: 어떡하지? 약이 없는데.

지연: 약국 아직 열**려 있**을까?

소연: 지금 11시 반이니까 아직   Since it's 11:30 now,
        열**려 있**을 거야.   it'll still be open.
        내가 빨리 가서 뭐 좀 사 올게.

(3) 손님: 와, 싱싱한 과일이 아주 많이   Wow! So many fresh
        나**와 있**네요!   fruits are out here.

주인: 네, 나온 지 얼마 안 돼요.
        좀 보실래요?

손님: 사과하고 배 좀 보여 주세요.

(4) 우진: 동수 씨, 밖에 누가 **와 있**어요. 나가 보세요.

동수: 누구예요?

우진: 잘 모르겠어요.

Notes

1. ~어/아 있다 expresses that a person or object is in a persistent state, typically resulting from a previous action designated by the verb. For example, apples being in a box in (1) is the result of someone having put them in the box. Similarly, in (4), 성희's being in the United States is the result of her having gone to the States. It should be noted, however, that what is focused with ~어/아 있다 is the current state of affairs, not the previous action that caused it.

2. The ~어/아 variation is the same as that of ~어요/아요, ~어서/아서, ~었/았, etc.

3. ~어/아 있다 is contrasted with ~고 있다, which expresses that a person or object is in a dynamic (progressive) process.

마이클이 의자에 앉고 있다.   마이클이 의자에 앉아 있다.

Describe the given pictures using ~어/아 있다.

   (1)   제임스가 의자에 _____

   (2)   스티브는 _____

   (3)   문이 _____

(4)   문이 _____

(5)   영어로 _____

(6)   리사가 침대에 _____
      (눕다 'to lie down')

✎ **Notes**

. . . .

. . . .

. . . .

. . . .

. . . .

. . . .

Conversation 2 여기 뭐 사러 왔어?

▌ 우진은 동네 슈퍼에서 우연히 수빈을 만났다.

Conversation 2

우진: 수빈아, 뭐 사러 왔어?

수빈: 응, 우유하고 빵하고 계란 좀 사러 왔어.
너도 여기 자주 오니?

우진: 아니, 보통은 서울마트에 가는데 오늘 좀
급해 가지고[G7.4] 몇 가지만 사려고 왔어.

수빈: 응. 뭐 사야 되는데?

우진: 치약이랑 칫솔이랑 비누 좀 사야 돼.
근데, 이번 주말에 친구들이 놀러 오는데
뭘 만들어 주면 좋을까?

수빈: 잡채 어때?

우진: 어 그거 좋다. 근데 잡채 만드는 데에[G7.5]
야채는 뭐뭐 들어가?

수빈: 보통 양파하고 당근, 시금치를 넣는데
나는 그냥 냉장고 열어 보고 있는 야채
다 집어 넣어.

우진: 그래, 그럼 한번 만들어 봐야겠다.

COMPREHENSION QUESTIONS

1. 수빈이는 슈퍼에서 무엇을 사려고 합니까?
2. 우진이는 슈퍼에서 무엇을 사려고 합니까?
3. 잡채에는 무엇이 들어갑니까?

NEW WORDS

NOUN

계란	egg	호박	pumpkin, squash
고기	meat	휴지	toilet paper
당근	carrot	**VERB**	
비누	soap	끓이다	to boil
빵	bread	넣다	to put in
시금치	spinach	들르다	to stop by
시장	market	싸우다	to fight
야채	vegetable	울다	to cry
양파	onion	웃다	to laugh
우유	milk	집어넣다	to put something in
잡채	*japchae*	**ADJECTIVE**	
치약	toothpaste	다양하다	to be diverse
칫솔	toothbrush	**SUFFIX**	
파	scallion	~(으)ㄴ/는 데에	in/for ~ing
편의점	convenience store	~어/아 가지고	because; by doing

NEW EXPRESSIONS

1. Several terms are used for stores where you can buy your daily groceries and other items, depending on the size of the store as well as the types of products they carry.

편의점	convenience store (e.g., 7-Eleven)
슈퍼마켓 (슈퍼)	market (e.g., small stores)
마트	mart (e.g., Walmart)

2. When a question includes more than one item to be taken as an answer, speakers duplicate some question words such as 뭐뭐, 어디어디, 누구누구.

> A: 파티에 누구누구 초대했어요?
>
> B: 마크랑 제니랑 린다를 초대했어요.

> A: 마트에서 뭐뭐 살 거예요?
>
> B: 빵이랑 우유랑 과일을 사야 돼요.

G7.4   ~어/아 가지고 'because, since'; 'by doing/being'

[Expressing a causal relation]

(1) 소연: 장 보러 자주 가?

   성희: 우리 냉장고가 작**아 가지고**,   Because our refrigerator is
       일주일에 두 번은 봐야 돼.   small, I have to come here
             twice a week.

(2) A: 보통 과일은 어디에서 사 먹어요?

   B: 시장이 너무 멀**어 가지고** 편의점에서 사요.

(3) A: 보통 어디서 장을 보세요?

   B: 물건이 싸고 다양**해 가지고** 마트에 자주 가는 편이에요.

[Expressing two sequential events]

(4) 동수: 고기는 누가 살 거예요?

   우진: 내가 **사 가지고** 갈게요.   I'll buy them (and take
             them to the party).

(5) 선생님:오늘 숙제 다 **해 가지고** 왔어요?

   민지: 숙제 있었어요? 저는 몰랐어요.

(6) 동수: 방학 동안 뭐 했어요?

   우진: 아르바이트 **해 가지고** 컴퓨터를 새로 샀어요.

Notes

1. 가지다 literally means 'to have/possess', but is idiomatized as 'with' or 'by' in ~어/아 가지고. ~어/아 가지고 is similar in usage to ~어/아서 in that both express two sequential events as in (1–3), and sometimes also a causal relation as in (4–6), where the first event triggers the second.

2. These functions of ~어/아 가지고 are similar to those of ~어서/아서. In fact it seems that in many instances, ~어 가지고 is replacing ~어서 in spoken language, limiting the use of ~어서/아서 to those cases where the two events conjoined are closely tied together. In the following examples, for instance, ~어서/아서 cannot be replaced with ~어/아 가지고.

> 늦어서 미안합니다.
> 머리가 아파서 먼저 집에 갈게요.
> 걸어서 학교에 가요.
> 집에 갈 때 빵집에 들러서 가세요.
>
> A: 어제 왜 병원에 갔어요?
> B: 배가 아파서 갔어요.

3. In speech, ~어/아 가지고 is pronounced as [어/아 가지구] or contracted to ~어/아 갖고, which is pronounced as [어/아 가꼬], [어/아 가꾸] or [어/아 각꾸].

Notes

· ·

· ·

· ·

· ·

· ·

· ·

Exercise

1. Using ~어/아 가지고, make up a dialogue according to the given context.

(1) A: 제니가 왜 울어요?

B: <u>동생하고 싸워 가지고</u> 우는 것 같아요.

(2) A: 어, 학교에 안 갔어요?

B: _____ 못 일어나겠어요.

(3) A: 사는 동네 어때요?

B: 이사온 지 _____ 잘 모르겠어요.
       1주일 전에 이사왔거든요.

(4) A: 새로 이사간 아파트 어때요?

B: _____ 조금 불편해요.
       시장이 조금 더 가까이 있으면 좋겠어요.

(5) A: 어제 파티에 왜 안 왔어요?

B: 미안해요. _____ 못 갔어요.

(6) A: 어디 가세요?

B: 휴지가 _____ 마트에 사러 가는 길이에요.

2. Say the following sentences using ~어/아 가지고.

(1) Please do your homework and bring it the day after tomorrow.

(2) Having studied economics in the United States, my older brother
     returned to Korea.

(3) Having not studied hard, my younger brother failed the
     college entrance exam.

3. Answer the following questions using ~어/아 가지고.

    (1) A: 이번 시험 잘 봤어?

          B: _____.

    (2) A: 어젯밤에 왜 전화했어?

          B: _____.

    (3) A: 김 선생님은 왜 하루 종일 웃으세요?

          B: _____.

    (4) A: 한국어를 왜 배우세요?

          B: _____.

G7.5　　~는 데(에) 'in/for ~ing . . .'

Examples

(1) 성희: 아주머니, 된장찌개 끓이는 데(에) 뭐가 들어가죠?   What goes in in making 된장찌개?

      주인: 두부하고 호박을 넣고, 파도 필요해요.

(2) 소연: 현대 소나타 하루 빌리는 데(에) 얼마예요?   How much is it for renting a Hyundai Sonata for one day?

      직원: 하루 삼만 원이에요.

(3) 주인: 지내는 데(에) 뭐 불편한 거 없어요?

      마크: 네, 없어요. 시장도 가깝고 교통도 편하고 다 좋아요. 전에는 장 보는 데(에) 세 시간이 걸렸는데, 지금은 30분이면 돼요.

(4) A: 시장이 여기서 멀어요?

      B: 아니요, 지하철 역까지 걸어 가는 데에만 한 20분 걸리고, 지하철만 타면 금방 가요.

Notes

1. 데 literally means a 'place', but 데 in ~는 데(에) refers to a place in a more abstract sense, that is, an activity or a situation. It can be best translated as 'in ~ing' or 'for ~ing'.

2. It should be noted that ~는 데 should be written with a space between 는 and 데, distinguished from ~는데, which refers to background circumstances.

Exercise

Find out from the given context what situation the people are up to, and make up a dialogue using ~는 데(에).

(1) A: <u>된장찌개 끓이는 데에 뭐뭐 넣어요?</u>
    B: 두부하고 호박을 넣고, 파도 넣어야 해요.

(2) A: _____?
    B: 하루 삼만 원이에요. 현대 소나타는 좀 비싸거든요.
        요즘은 엘란트라도 많이 빌리는데 지금은 없어요.

(3) [A is going to a dance party.]
    A: _____ 어떤 옷이 어울려요?
    B: 검정색이나 하늘색이 어때요?

(4) A: 아, 배 아파. 약 있으면 좀 줄래?
    B: 여기 있어.
    A: 이거 말고 다른 거 없어?
    B: 왜? _____는 이 약이 제일 좋아.

(5) [스티브 moved in just a few days ago.]
    하숙집 주인: _____ 불편한 거 없어요?
    스티브: 네, 없어요. 다 좋아요.

Narration	동네 시장

우진이는 한 달 전에 지금 사는 원룸으로 이사를 왔다.
기숙사에서는 장 보는 것이 불편했는데 지금 사는 집에서는
큰 길을 건너면 바로 그 앞에 시장이 있어서 편하다. 시장에는
큰 슈퍼마켓, 과일 가게, 야채 가게, 생선 가게, 정육점[1], 빵집도
있고, 옷 가게, 신발 가게, 화장품 가게, 약국 등이 있어서
필요한 물건들을 쉽게 살 수 있다. 물건 값도 백화점보다
싼 편이다. 물건을 많이 사면 배달도 해 주기 때문에 아주
편리하다. 동네 시장 안에는 편의점도 하나 있는데 24시간
열려 있어서 늦은 시간에도 필요한 물건을 살 수 있다.

1. 정육점: butcher's shop

COMPREHENSION QUESTIONS

1. 우진이는 언제 지금 사는 아파트로 이사왔습니까?
2. 지금 사는 아파트에서 시장에 가려면 어떻게 합니까?
3. 슈퍼마켓은 왜 편리합니까?
4. 어디서 배달을 해 줍니까?

CULTURE

택배

물건[1]을 배달할 때 요즘 한국 사람들이 가장 많이 사용하는 서비스는 택배[2]다. 택배로 물건을 받기도 하고 보내기도 한다. 택배로 물건을 받을 때는 택배 기사에게 사인[3]을 해 주어야 한다.

인터넷 쇼핑을 할 때도 택배로 물건을 받는다. 백화점에서 옷이나 신발을 사고 나서 수선[4]을 했을 때 택배로 집에 배달이 된다. 추석이나 설날, 크리스마스 같은 때에는 많은 사람들이 택배 서비스를 사용하기 때문에 배달 시간이 다른 때보다 좀 더 오래 걸릴 수 있지만, 보통 때는 하루나 이틀이면 원하는[5] 곳으로 물건들을 배달 시킬 수 있다.

1. 물건: articles, goods
2. 택배: delivery service
3. 사인: sign
4. 수선: alteration
5. 원하다: to want

USAGE

1 *Talking about food and making a shopping list*

(1) (성희 and 소연 run into each other at a supermarket.)

성희: 소연아, 여기 웬일이니? 뭐 사러 왔니?

소연: 응, 휴지도 사고 또 오렌지 주스랑 과일 좀 사러 왔어.
너도 장 보러 왔니?

성희: 응, 난 집에서 밥을 해 먹으니까 살 게 많아.

소연: 오늘 저녁 메뉴가 뭔데?

성희: 된장찌개 끓이려고. 감자 (potatoes), 호박, 양파, 마늘
(garlic), 콩나물 (bean sprouts) 샀어.
아, 참. 시금치하고 계란도 사야 되는데.

소연: 그럼, 어서 장 봐.

성희: 그래, 또 보자. 잘 가.

(2) 주인: 어서 오세요. 뭘 드릴까요?

성희: 감자하고 파 좀 주세요.

주인: 감자는 몇 개 드릴까요?

성희: 4개 주세요. 파는 두 단 주세요.
참, 그리고 콩나물도 한 봉지 주세요.

Locating items at a supermarket

_____이/가 어디 있어요?

Inquiring about the price of items at a grocery store.

오렌지 하나에 얼마예요?
사과 한 상자에 얼마예요?

⬤ **Exercise 1**

Practice the above conversation (1) and make a shopping list for 성희 and 소연.

소연's shopping list   성희's shopping list

_____   _____

_____   _____

_____   _____

_____   _____

Read your list to your class.

⬤ **Exercise 2**

Look at 우진's shopping list below and role-play a conversation between 우진 and the grocer.

> 시장 볼 것들 (shopping list)
> 소고기 500그램
> 감자 4 개
> 콩나물 1 봉지
> 사과 한 상자
> 호박 큰 것 두 개
> 파 두 단
> 과일
> 고추장 작은 것 하나

⬤ **Exercise 3**

Write a grocery list for yourself.

▌ **Exercise 4**

Exchange the following information with a classmate.

(1) 시장 보러 얼마나 자주 가세요?

(2) 어느 슈퍼마켓에 잘 가세요?

(3) 생선(fish)을 좋아하세요, 고기를 좋아하세요?

(4) 야채 많이 드세요?

(5) 무슨 과일을 제일 좋아하세요?

(6) 저녁에 보통 뭐 먹어요?

▌ **Exercise 5**

Role-play the following situations.

(1) Your roommate is going to go to the Korean market in town. Ask him or her to buy some Korean food for you.

(2) You are at the Korean supermarket, and you want to know the price of a product and where to find it at the market.

✎ **Notes**

. . . .

. . . .

. . . .

. . . .

. . . .

. . . .

2 *Making recipes*

(1) [불고기 샌드위치 만들기]
   재료: 빵, 쇠고기, 간장 1큰술, 설탕 1/2큰술, 참기름 1/2작은술
   　　　파, 마늘 1작은술, 후추 약간, 상추 2장, 토마토 2개

   만드는 법:
   ① 소고기를 얇게 썰어 간장, 설탕, 참기름, 파, 마늘, 후추를
   　넣어 양념한다.
   ② 팬을 뜨겁게 달구어 양념한 불고기를 넣어 볶는다.
   ③ 상추는 씻는다.
   ④ 토마토는 얇게 썰어 둔다.
   ⑤ 빵 위에 상추와 토마토를 깔고 그 위에 불고기를 얹는다.

(2) [라면 만들기]
   ① 끓는 물 (3컵 정도)에 면과 스프를 넣고 4-5 분간 더
   　끓이면 맛있는 라면이 됩니다.
   ② 식성에 따라 김치, 계란, 파 등을 넣어 드시면 더 맛이 좋습니다.

Examples

Useful words

소고기 beef, 간장 soy sauce, 설탕 sugar, 참기름 sesame oil, 파 green onions,
마늘 garlic, 후추 black pepper, 상추 lettuce, 토마토 tomatoes, 큰술 tablespoon,
만드는 법 recipe, 얇게 썰다 thin slice, 양념하다 to season, 팬 pan, 달구다 to heat,
볶다 to stir-fry, 씻다 to wash, 두다 to put aside, 깔다 to spread, 얹다 to put on top,
끓다 to boil, 면 noodles, 수프 soup base, 식성 appetite, 에 따라 according to

Notes

. . . .

. . . .

. . . .

. . . .

Exercise 1

Converse with your partner about the recipe above.

> **Examples**
>
> A: 불고기 만드는 데에 무슨 재료가 필요해요?
> B: 쇠고기, 간장, 설탕, 참기름, 파, 마늘, 후추가 필요해요.

Exercise 2

Describe your favorite recipe in Korean.

3 Expressing hesitation

> (At a clothing store)
> 점원: 손님, 이게 요새 유행하는 스타일이에요.
>   이걸 한번 입어 보세요.
> 손님: 글쎄요. (implying "I am not quite comfortable with this
>   style.")
>   이런 스타일은 한번도 안 입어 봐서 어떨지 모르겠어요.
> 점원: 그럼, 이런 스타일은 어떠세요?
> 손님: 색깔이 좀 . . . (expressing some reservation about the color)

You can express your reservations in various contexts. Hesitation devices give you time to think and to respond in a polite manner. There are various linguistic devices in Korean to express one's reservations. For example,

저어/저 (with a hesitant tone)	uh, um
저기요	Excuse me.
음	uh, um
글쎄요	Well, I am not quite sure.
사실은요	in fact, to tell you the truth
있잖아요.	you know

You can use hesitation devices in the following situations.

(1) To get the attention of a stranger
저어 (as a conversation opener)
실례합니다. 말씀 좀 묻겠습니다.

(2) To call a customer
저기요 'Excuse me'.
손님, 거스름돈 받아 가셔야지요.

(3) To make a request or ask a favor
저 (with a hesitant tone), 미안하지만, 부탁이 하나 있는데요.

(4) When expressing one's opinion
Another way of expressing one's reservation is to use
incomplete sentences as in the model dialogue in the box
above (e.g., 색깔이 좀 . . .).

Exercise

Role-play the following situations. Use some of the hesitation devices listed
above. Don't use silence to express hesitation.

(1) You're calling out to a stranger who has forgotten her purse on a chair.

(2) You want to ask a stranger on the street for directions to the nearest
post office.

(3) You visit your Korean professor's office without an appointment and
find that she or he is busy.

Lesson 7 At a store

CONVERSATION 1   *How much is one box of apples?*

Woojin went to the fruit store in his neighborhood to buy fruits.

Woojin: How are you, ma'am?

Owner: Oh, long time no see. Have you been somewhere all this time?

Woojin: Yes, I was at my home in the United States during the vacation.

Owner: You were?

Woojin: Wow! These fruits look delicious. Which fruit sells well these days?

Owner: Apples and pears tend to sell well.

Woojin: How much is one box of apples?

Owner: It is 20,000 won.

Woojin: How many apples are there in one box?

Owner: There are ten.

Woojin: These tangerines also look delicious. How much are the tangerines?

Owner: It is 1,000 won for three.

Woojin: Then, please give me 3,000 won's worth.

CONVERSATION 2   *What did you come here to buy?*

Woojin met Soobin at the market by chance.

Woojin: Soobin, what did you come to buy?

Soobin: Well, I'm going to buy milk, bread, and eggs. Do you come here often?

Woojin: No, usually I go to the big mart. However, I'm here because I urgently need to buy a few things.

Soobin: I see. What do you have to buy?

Woojin: I am going to buy toothpaste, a toothbrush, and soap. By the way, what vegetables do I need for making *japchae*?

Soobin: They usually put in onions, carrots, and spinach, but I just open the refrigerator and put in any vegetables that I have.

Woojin: Okay. I will try making it this weekend.

NARRATION　　*Market in the neighborhood*

Woojin moved into a studio one month ago, which is where he now lives. It used to be inconvenient to go grocery shopping when he lived at the dormitory, but now, grocery shopping is convenient because there is a market directly across the big road from where he lives. It is easy to buy necessary items at the marketplace because there is a big supermarket, fruit store, vegetable store, fish store, butcher, and bakery as well as a clothing store, shoe store, cosmetics store, pharmacy, and so on. The prices are on the cheap side when compared to those of department stores. It is very convenient because the shops have delivery service for those who buy a lot. Especially convenient is the convenience store at the marketplace in the neighborhood. He can buy items at any time there because it is open twenty-four hours a day.

CULTURE　　택배

택배 is the most popular service when Korean people deliver articles these days. People receive and send articles using 택배. When you receive an article by 택배, you need to sign for it.

You receive items that you shopped for online by 택배. Clothes or shoes that you bought at the department store are delivered to your house through 택배 after alteration. Usually you can expect delivery in one or two days except on days like Thanksgiving or New Year's Day or Christmas when many people use 택배 service and delivery takes a little longer than usual.

Grammar Index

Item	Meaning	Lesson
~(으)ㄴ/는지 알다/모르다	to know/not know whether	Lesson 5 C1
~(으)니까	expresses reason	Lesson 3 C2
~(으)려고 하다	intend to	Lesson 2 C1
~(으)려면	if . . . intends to	Lesson 4 C2
~(으)면 되다	all one needs is	Lesson 3 C1
~(으)면 좋겠다	I wish	Lesson 1 C2
~잖아요	you know	Lesson 1 C1

Korean-English Glossary

1학년	freshman
2학년	sophomore
3학년	junior
4학년	senior
가	subject particle
가게	store
가격	price
가구	furniture
가구점	furniture store
가깝다	to be close, near
가끔	sometimes
가다	to go
가르치다	to teach
가방	bag
가볍다	to be light
가수	singer
가운데	the middle, the center
가위, 바위, 보	rock-paper-scissors
가을	autumn, fall
가장	the most
가져가다	to take, carry
가족	family
각	each
간장	soy sauce
간판	store signs
갈비	*kalbi* (spareribs)
갈아 입다	to change (clothes)
갈아 타다	to change (vehicles)
감기에 걸리다	to have/catch a cold
감사하다	to be thankful
감자	potato
갑자기	suddenly
값	price
강원	Gangwon region
갖고 가다	to take
갖고 다니다	to carry around
갖고 오다	to bring
갖다 놓다	to bring and put down somewhere
갖다	to bring/take
드리다*hum.*	something to someone
갖다 주다*plain*	to bring/take something to someone
같이	together
개	1. dog; 2. item (counter)
개월	month
거	thing (contraction of 것)
거기	there
거리	1. distance; 2. street, avenue
거스름돈	change (money)
거실	living room
거의	almost
걱정	worry, concern
걱정하다	to worry
건강하다	to be healthy
건너다	to cross
건너편	the other side
건물	building
건조하다	to be dry
건축물	building, structure
건축학	architecture
걷다	to walk
걸다	to call
걸리다	to take [time]
걸어가다	to go on foot
걸어다니다	to walk around
걸어오다	to come on foot
검정색	black
것	thing (=거)
게임	game
겨울	winter
결혼	marriage
결혼식	wedding
결혼하다	to get married
경기	match, game
경우	case
경제학	economics
경주	Gyeongju
경찰	police
경찰서	police station
경치	scenery, view
경험	experience
계단	stairs
계란	egg
계산서	check
계속	continuously
계속되다	to continue
계시다*hon.*	to be (existence), stay
계절	season
계좌	account
계획	plan

계획하다	to plan	구두	dress shoes
고기	meat	구두 시험	oral exam
고등학교	high school	구름	cloud
고등학생	high school student	구름이 끼다	to get cloudy
고르다	to choose, select	구하다	to search for
고맙다	to be thankful	국경일	national holidays
고생	hardship	국내선	domestic flight
고생하다	to have a difficult time	국제선	international flight
고속도로	highway, freeway	국제 전화	international call
고장	breakdown	군데	place, spot
고장나다	to break down	굽	heel
고추장	red-pepper paste	권	volume (counter)
고층빌딩	high-rise building	귀걸이	earring
고향	hometown	귤	tangerine
곧	right away, soon	그	that
골동품	antique	그냥	just, without any special reason
골프	golf		
곳	place	그동안	meantime
공	0 (zero: for phone #)	그래서	so, therefore
공기	air	그램	gram
공부	study	그러면	then, in that case
공부방	study room	그런데	1. but, however; 2. by the way
공부하다	to study		
공사	construction	그럼	(if so) then
공예품	craftwork	그렇다	to be so
공원	park	그렇지만	but, however
공장	factory	그릇	dish
공포 영화	horror movie	그리고	and
공항	airport	그리다	to draw
과	1. lesson, chapter; 2. and (joins nouns)	그림	picture, painting
		그립다	to miss, long for
과목	course, subject	그만	without doing anything further
과일	fruit		
과자	cracker	극장	movie theater
과학	science	근처	nearby, vicinity
관악산	Gwanak Mountain	글쎄요	Well; It's hard to say
괜찮다	to be all right, okay	금반지	gold ring
굉장히	very much	금방	soon
교과서	textbook	금요일	Friday
교복	school uniform	기계 공학	mechanical engineering
교수님	professor	기다려지다	to be wished
교실	classroom	기다리다	to wait
교육학	education	기분	feeling
교통	traffic	기쁘다	to be joyful, glad
교통 표지판	traffic sign	기사	driver
교통카드	transportation card	기숙사	dormitory
교회	church	기억	memory
구경	sightseeing	기억하다	to remember
구경하다	to look around; to sightsee	기온	temperature
		기원전	B.C.

기차	train	남동생	younger brother
기타	guitar	남미	South America
길	1. street, road	남부	southern
	2. way	남산	Nam Mountain
길다	to be long	남색	navy blue, indigo
김밥	*kimbap*	남아있다	to remain
김치	kimchi	남자	man
까만색	black (=까망)	낮	daytime
까맣다	to be black	낮다	to be low
까지	1. up to (location);	낮아지다	to get lower
	2. to/until/through (time);	내*plain*	my (=제*hum.*)
		내년	next year
	3. including	내다	1. to pay (money);
깎다	to cut down		2. to turn in
깔다	to spread		(homework)
깨끗하다	to be clean	내려가다	to go down
깨지다	to break	내리다	to get off
께*hon.*	to (a person)	내일	tomorrow
께서*hon.*	subject particle (=이/가 *plain*)	냉면	*naengmyŏn* (cold buckwheat noodles)
꼭	surely, certainly	냉장고	refrigerator
꽃	flower	너	you *plain*
꽃집	flower shop	너무	too much
꿈(을) 꾸다	to dream a dream	넓다	to be spacious, wide
끓이다	to boil	넘어지다	to fall (down)
끝나다	to be over, finished	넣다	to put in
끼다	to be foggy	네	1. yes;
끼다	to wear (glasses, gloves, rings)		2. I see; 3. okay
나*plain*	I (=저*hum.*)	네거리	intersection
나가다	to go out	넥타이	necktie
나다	happen, break out	년	year (counter)
나라	country	노란색	yellow
나쁘다	to be bad	노랗다	to be yellow
나오다	to come out	노래	song
나이	age	노래 부르다	to sing
나이가 들다	to gain age	노래하다	to sing
나중에	later	노래방	karaoke room
나타내다	to show, represent	녹차	green tea
나흘	four days	놀다	to play; to not work
난방	heating	놀라다	to be surprised
날	day	농구	basketball
날마다	every day	농구하다	to play basketball
날씨	weather	농구 시합	basketball game
날씬하다	to be thin	농사	farming
날짜	date	높다	to be high
남	south	놓아 주다	to put something down for someone
남기다	to leave (a message)	누가	1. who (누구+가);
남다	to remain		2. someone

누구	1. who;
	2. someone
누나	the older sister of a male
눈(이) 오다	to snow
눈	1. eyes;
	2. snow
눕다	to lie down
뉴스	news
뉴욕	New York
는	topic particle ('as for')
늘다	to improve
늦게	late
늦다	to be late
늦잠	oversleep
다	all
다녀 오다	to go and get back
다니다	1. to attend;
	2. to get around
다르다	to be different
다보탑	Dabo Tower
다소	more or less; to some degree
다시	again
다양하다	to be diverse
다음	next, following
다음부터(는)	from next time
다치다	to hurt
단	bundle; bunch
단어	vocabulary
단정하다	to be neat
단풍	fall foliage
닫다	to close
닫히다	to be closed
달	1. month (counter);
	2. moon
달구다	to heat
달다	to be sweet
달러	dollar (=불)
달력	calendar
닮다	to resemble
담배	cigarette
답	answer
답장	reply
답장하다	to reply
당근	carrot
대답	answer
대답하다	to answer
대중	the public

대체로	generally, mostly
대충	roughly
대통령	president
대통령 선거	presidential election
대학	college, university
대학교	college, university
대학생	college student
대학원	graduate school
대학원생	graduate student
대한항공	Korean Air
대해서	about
댁*hon.*	home, house (=집*plain*)
더	more
더럽다	to be dirty
덜	less
덥다	to be hot
덮다	to close, cover
데	place
데이트	a date
데이트하다	to date
도	1. also, too;
	2. degree
도둑	thief
도서관	library
도시	city
도와 드리다*hon.*	to help
도와 주다*plain*	to help
도움	help
도착하다	to arrive
도쿄	Tokyo
독방	single room
독서	reading
독서하다	to read
돈	money
돈을 내다	to pay
돈을 벌다	to earn money
돈이 들다	to cost money
돌	the first birthday
돌다	to turn
돌려 드리다*hum.*	to return (something to someone)
돌려 주다*plain*	to return (something to someone)
돌아가다	to return (to)
돌아가시다*hon.*	to pass away
돌아오다	to return, come back
돕다	to help
동	east
동남아	Southeast Asia

동네	neighborhood	라면	instant noodles (ramen)
동대문시장	Dongdaemun Market	라운지	lounge
동물원	zoo	램프	lamp
동부	East Coast	랩	lab
동생	younger sibling	러시아	Russia
동안	during	런던	London
동양학	Asian studies	로스앤젤레스	Los Angeles (L.A.)
되다	1. to become;	록	rock music
	2. get, turn into;	룸메이트	roommate
	3. to function, work	를	object particle
된장찌개	soybean-paste stew	마늘	garlic
두	two (with counter)	마당	yard
두 번째	the second	마르다	to be skinny
두껍다	to be thick	마리	animal (counter)
두부	tofu	마시다	to drink
둘	two	마을 버스	town shuttle bus
뒤	the back, behind	마음	mind, heart
드라마	drama	마음에 들다	to be to one's liking
드럼	drum	마중 나가다	to go out to greet
드리다*hum.*	to give (=주다*plain*)		someone
드시다*hon.*	to eat (=먹다*plain*)	마중 나오다	to come out to greet
듣다	1. to listen;		someone
	2. to take a course	마침	just, just in time
들	plural particle	마켓	market
들르다	to stop by	마트	mart
들어가다	to enter	막내	youngest child
들어오다	to come in	막히다	to be blocked, congested
들어있다	to contain	만	only
등	et cetera	만나다	to meet
등기	registered (mail)	만드는 법	recipe
등산	hiking	만들다	to make
등산객	mountain climber	만화방	comic book rental store
등산하다	to hike	만화책	comic book
따님*hon.*	daughter	많다	to be many, much
따뜻하다	to be warm	많이	much, many
따라하다	to repeat after	말	speech, words
딸	daughter	말고	not N1 but N2
때	time	말씀*hon.*	speech, words (=말 *plain*)
때문에	because of	말하다	to speak
떠나다	to leave	맑다	to be clear
또	and, also, too	맛보다	to taste
똑같다	to be identical	맛없다	to be tasteless, not
똑바로	straight, upright		delicious
뚱뚱하다	to be fat	맛있다	to be delicious
뛰다	to run	맞다	1. to fit;
뜨겁다	to be hot		2. to be correct
뜨다	to rise; to come up	매년	every year
뜻하다	to mean, signify	매다	to tie
라디오	radio	매달	every month

매일	every day	무엇	what (=뭐)
매주	every week	무척	very much
매표소	ticket office	문	door
맵다	to be spicy	문제	problem
머리	1. head;	문학	literature
	2. hair	문화	culture
먹거리	things to eat	묻다	to ask
먹다	to eat	물	water
먼저	first, beforehand	물가	cost of living
멀다	to be far	물건	merchandise, stuff
멋있다	to be stylish, attractive	물다	to bite
메뉴	menu	물리다	to be bitten
메시지	message	물리학	physics
멕시코	Mexico	물어보다	to inquire
며칠	1. what date;	물품	articles, goods
	2. a few days	뭐	1. what (=무엇);
면	noodles		2. something
명	people (counter)	미국	the United States
명절	traditional holidays	미안하다	to be sorry
몇	how many, what (with	미용실	beauty salon
	a counter)	미터기	meter
모두	all	밑	the bottom, below
모레	the day after tomorrow	바겐 세일	bargain sale
모르다	to not know, be	바꾸다	to change, switch
	unaware of	바뀌다	to be changed
모양	shape	바다	sea
모으다	to collect	바닥	floor
모이다	to gather	바닷가	beach
모자	cap, hat	바람	wind
모자라다	to lack	바로	directly
모텔	motel	바빠지다	to get busier
목(이) 마르다	to be thirsty	바쁘다	to be busy
목걸이	necklace	바이올린	violin
목도리	muffler, scarf	바지	pants
목소리	voice	박물관	museum
목요일	Thursday	박스	box
목욕	bath	밖	outside
목욕하다	to bathe	밖에	nothing but, only
몸	body	반	1. class;
몸조리	care of health		2. half
못	cannot	반갑다	to be glad
못생기다	to be ugly	반값	half price
무겁다	to be heavy	반드시	surely, certainly
무게	weight	반바지	shorts
무덥다	to be hot and humid	반지	ring
무료	free of charge	반찬	side dishes
무섭다	to be scary; scared	받다	to receive
무슨	1. what, what kind of;	발	foot
	2. some kind of	발달	development

발달하다	to develop, grow	볼거리	things to watch
발매기	vending machine	볼링	bowling
밝다	to be bright	볼펜	ballpoint pen
밤	night	봄	spring
밥	1. cooked rice;	봉지	pack; bag
	2. meal	봉투	envelope
방	room	뵙다 *hum.*	to see (=보다 *plain*)
방금	a moment ago	부르다 (노래)	to sing (a song)
방송국	broadcasting station	부모님	parents
방학	school vacation	부엌	kitchen
배	1. stomach, abdomen;	부자	a wealthy person
	2. pear	부족하다	to be insufficient
배(가) 고프다	to be hungry	부치다	to mail (a letter, parcel)
배(가) 부르다	to have a full stomach	부탁하다	to ask a favor
배달	delivery	부터	from (time) . . .
배달하다	to deliver	북	north
배우다	to learn	분	minute (counter)
배터리	battery	분 *hon.*	people (=명 *plain*)
백만	million	불	dollar (=달러)
백화점	department store	불고기	*pulgogi* (roast meat)
밴쿠버	Vancouver	불교	Buddhism
버스	bus	불국사	Pulgugsa
번	1. number (counter);	불다	to blow
	2. number of times	불편하다	to be uncomfortable,
	(e.g., 한 번)		inconvenient
번째	ordinal numbers	붙이다	to stick, affix
번호	number	브로드웨이	Broadway theater
벌	a pair of (counter)	극장	
벌다	to earn (money)	블라우스	blouse
벌써	already	비	rain
법학	law	비(가) 오다	to rain
벗다	to take off, undress	비교적	relatively
별	star	비누	soap
별로	not really/particularly	비빔밥	*pibimbap* (rice with
병원	hospital		vegetables and beef)
보내다	1. to spend time;	비슷하다	to be similar
	2. to send	비싸다	to be expensive
보다	to see, look, watch	비자	visa
보다	than	비행기	airplane
보스톤	Boston	빌딩	building
보이다	to be seen, visible	빌려주다	to lend
보통	1. usually;	빌리다	to borrow
	2. regular	빠르다	to be fast
복	good fortune	빨간색	red
복도	aisle	빨갛다	to be red
복습	review	빨래하다	to do the laundry
복잡하다	to be crowded	빨리	fast, quickly
볶다	to stir-fry	빵	bread
본인 확인	self-identification	뺏기다	to be deprived of

사	4
사 먹다	to buy and eat
사거리	intersection
사고	accident
사과	apple
사귀다	1. to make friends; 2. to date
사다	to buy
사람	person, people
사랑	love
사랑하다	to love
사모님	teacher's wife
사무실	office
사실	fact, truth
사용하다	to use
사우나	sauna
사이	1. relationship; 2. between
사이즈	size
사인	sign
사전	dictionary
사진	photo, picture
사찰	temple
사투리	dialect
사회보장번호	Social Security number
사흘	three days
살	1. years old; 2. flesh, fat
살다	to live
삼	3
상	table
상가	shopping district
상자	box
상점	store
상추	lettuce
새	new
새로	newly
새벽	dawn
새해	New Year
색	color (=색깔)
샌드위치	sandwich
샌들	sandals
생기다	to be formed
생년월일	date of birth
생물학	biology
생선	fish
생신hon.	birthday
생일	birthday
생활	daily life, living

샤워	shower
샤워하다	to take a shower
서	west
서기	A.D.
서다	to stand
서두르다	to hurry
서랍	drawer
서로	each other
서비스	service
서울	Seoul
서울대입구역	Seoul National University Station
서울타워	Seoul Tower
서점	bookstore (=책방)
석가탑	Seokga Tower
석굴암	Seokguram (stone cave)
선물	present, gift
선물하다	to give a present, gift
선생님	teacher
설거지	dishwashing
설거지하다	to wash dishes
설악산	Seorak Mount
설탕	sugar
섬	island
섭씨	Celsius
성격	personality
성별	sex, gender
성적	grade
성함hon.	name (=이름plain)
세기	century
세수하다	to wash one's face
세우다	to stop, pull over
세일	sale
세탁기	washing machine
세탁소	laundry, cleaners
세트	a set
센트	cent
셔츠	shirt
소개	introduction
소개하다	to introduce
소고기	beef
소극적이다	to be passive
소리	sound, noise
소매	sleeve
소방서	fire station
소설	novel
소파	sofa
소포	parcel, package
손	hand

손(을) 씻다	to wash one's hands	시원해지다	to become cooler
손님	guest, customer	시작하다	to begin
쇼	show	시장	marketplace
쇼핑	shopping	시청	city hall
쇼핑하다	to shop	시청역	city hall station
수고하다	to put forth effort, take trouble	시카고	Chicago
		시키다	to order (food)
수도	capital city	시합	game, match
수선	alteration	시험	test, exam
수업	course, class	식당	restaurant
수영	swimming	식비	food expenses
수영장	swimming pool	식사	meal
수영하다	to swim	식사하다	to have a meal
수요일	Wednesday	식성	appetite
수저	spoon and chopsticks	식탁	dining table
수프	soup	신기하다	to be amazing
숙제	homework	신나다	to be excited
숙제하다	to do homework	신다	to wear (footwear)
순두부찌개	soft tofu stew	신라	Silla
숟가락	spoon	신문	newspaper
술	alcoholic beverage	신문사	newspaper publisher
술집	pub, bar	신발	shoes
숫자	number	신분증	identification card
쉬다	to rest	신용 카드	credit card
쉽다	to be easy	신호등	traffic light
슈퍼(마켓)	supermarket	실	thread
스릴러	thriller	실례하다	to be excused
스시	sushi	싫다	to be undesirable
스웨터	sweater	싫어하다	to dislike
스키	ski	심리학	psychology
스키 타다	to ski	심심하다	to be bored
스타일	style	싱겁다	to be bland
스트레스	stress	싶다	to want to
스파게티	spaghetti	싸다	1. to be cheap;
스페인	Spain		2. to wrap;
스포츠	sports		3. to pack
슬리퍼	slipper	싸우다	to fight
슬프다	to be sad	썰다	to slice
승차권	ride pass, ticket	쓰다	1. to write;
시	hour, o'clock		2. to use;
시간	time, hour (duration)		3. to wear headgear;
시계	clock, watch		4. to be bitter
시금치	spinach	쓰이다	to be used
시끄럽다	to be noisy	씨	attached to a person's name for courtesy
시내	downtown		
시다	to be sour	아	oh
시대	period	아까	a while ago
시드니	Sydney	아니다	to not be (negative equation)
시원하다	to be cool, refreshing		

아니요	no	약국	drugstore
아들	son	약도	map
아래층	downstairs	약속	1. engagement;
아르바이트	part-time job		2. promise
아름답다	to be beautiful	얇게	thinly
아마	probably, perhaps	얇다	to be thin
아버지	father	양념	condiment, seasoning
아쉽다	to be sad, feel the lack of	양념하다	to season
아시아	Asia	양력	solar calendar
아이	child	양말	socks, stockings
아이스크림	ice cream	양식	Western-style (food)
아이스하키	ice hockey	양파	onion
아저씨	mister; a man of one's	얘기	talk, chat (=이야기)
	parents' age	얘기하다	to talk, chat
아주	very, really	어	oh
아주머니	middle-aged woman	어느	which
아직	yet, still	어둡다	to be dark
아직도	yet, still	어디	1. what place, where;
아침	1. breakfast;		2. somewhere
	2. morning	어떤	which, what kind of
아파트	apartment	어떻게	how
아프다	to be sick	어떻다	to be how
악기	musical instrument	어렵다	to be difficult
안	1. the inside;	어른	adult, (one's) elders
	2. do not	어리다	to be young
안개	fog	어머	Oh! Oh my! Dear me!
안경	eyeglasses	어머니	mother
안녕하다	to be well	어서	quick(ly)
안녕히	in peace	어업	fishery
안방	master bedroom	어울리다	to match, suit
안부	regards	어제	yesterday
안전하다	to be safe	어젯밤	last night
앉다	to sit	어치	worth, value
않다	to not be, to not do	언니	the older sister of a
알다	to know		female
알래스카	Alaska	언어학	linguistics
알리다	to inform	언제	1. when;
알아듣다	to understand, recognize		2. sometime
알아보다	to find out, check out	얹다	to put
앞	the front	얼굴	face
액세서리	accessory	얼다	to freeze
액션	action	얼마	how long/much
야구	baseball	얼마나	how long/much
야구하다	to play baseball	얼음	ice
야구장	baseball stadium	엄마	mom
야외	the outside	없다	1. to not be (existence);
야채	vegetable		2. to not have
약	1. approximately;	없어지다	to disappear
	2. medicine		

에	1. in, at, on (static location);
	2. to (destination);
	3. at, in, on (time);
	4. for, per
에 따라	according to
에서	1. in, at (dynamic location);
	2. from (location);
	3. from (time)
에어컨	air-conditioner
엘리베이터	elevator
여권	passport
여기	here
여동생	younger sister
여러	many, several
여름	summer
여보	honey, dear
여보세요	hello (on the phone)
여자	woman
여자 친구	girlfriend
여행	travel, trip
여행사	travel agency
여행하다	to travel
역	station
역사	history
연결	connection, link
연결하다	to connect, link
연구실	professor's office
연극	play, drama
연락	contact
연락하다	to contact
연세 *hon.*	age (=나이 *plain*)
연습	practice
연습 문제	exercise
연습하다	to practice
연주	musical performance
연주하다	to perform on a musical instrument
연필	pencil
열다	to open
열리다	to be open
열쇠	key
열심히	diligently
엽서	postcard
영	0 (zero)
영국	the United Kingdom
영서	Yeongseo region
영수증	receipt
영어	the English language

영하	below the freezing point
영화	movie
옆	the side, beside
예	yes, I see, okay (=네)
예를 들어	for example
예쁘다	to be pretty
예술	art
예약	reservation
예약하다	to reserve
옛날	the old days
오늘	today
오다	to come
오래	long time
오래간만	after a long time
오랫동안	for a long time
오른쪽	right side
오빠	the older brother of a female
오전	a.m.
오페라	opera
오후	afternoon
온돌	floor heating system
올라가다	to go up
올림	sincerely yours
올림픽	Olympics
올해	this year
옮기다	to move, shift
옷	clothes
옷가게	clothing store
옷장	wardrobe, closet
와	1. and (joins nouns);
	2. Wow!
와이셔츠	dress shirt
왕복	round-trip
왜	why
외국	foreign country
외국어	foreign language
외국인	foreigner
외국인등록번호	Alien Registration number
외롭다	to be lonely
외식하다	to eat out
외우다	to memorize
왼쪽	left side
요금	fee, fare
요리	cooking
요리하다	to cook
요새	these days
요즘	these days

우리*plain*	we/us/our (=저희*hum.*)	음식값	food cost
우산	umbrella	음식점	restaurant (=식당)
우연히	by chance, accident	음악	music
우유	milk	음악회	concert
우체국	post office	응	yeah
우체부	postman	의	of
우체통	postbox	의사	doctor
우편	mail service	의생활	clothing habits
우편 번호	postal code	의자	chair
우편 요금	postage	이(를) 닦다	to brush one's teeth
우표	stamp	이	1. 2;
운	luck, fortune		2. subject particle;
운동	exercise		3. this;
운동장	playground		4. a suffix inserted
운동하다	to exercise		after a Korean first
운동화	sports shoes, sneakers		name that ends in a
운전	driving		consonant;
운전 면허	driver's license		5. tooth
운전하다	to drive	이거	this (=이것)
울다	to cry	이기다	to win
웃다	to laugh	이다	to be (equation)
원 (₩)	won (Korean currency)	이따가	a little later
원룸	studio apartment	이름	name
원피스	(one-piece) dress	이메일	e-mail
원하다	to wish, want	이발소	barbershop
월	month (counter)	이번	this time
월드컵	World Cup	이사하다	to move
월요일	Monday	이스트 홀	East Hall
웬일	what matter	이야기	talk, chat (=얘기)
위	the top side, above	이야기하다	to talk (=얘기하다)
위험하다	to be dangerous	이용하다	to utilize
유난히	particularly	이젠	now (이제+는)
유니온 빌딩	Union Building	이쪽으로	this way + 으로
유니폼	uniform	이태리	Italy
유럽	Europe	이틀	two days
유명하다	to be famous	이해하다	to understand
유학생	student abroad	익숙하다	to be familiar
유행	fashion, trend	인구	population
유행하다	to be in fashion	인기	popularity
육개장	hot shredded-beef soup	인도	sidewalk
으로	1. by means of;	인사	greeting
	2. toward, to;	인사하다	to greet
	3. item selected among	인사동	Insadong
	many other options	인사하다	to greet
은	topic particle ('as for')	인상적	memorable
은행	bank	인천	Incheon
을	object particle	인터넷	Internet
음력	lunar calendar	인터뷰	interview
음료수	beverage	일 인 분	one portion
음식	food		

일	1. 1;
	2. day (counter);
	3. work;
	4. event
일기	journal
일기예보	weather forecast
일등석	first-class seat
일반석	economy-class seat
일본	Japan
일식	Japanese food
일어나다	to get up
일요일	Sunday
일찍	early
일하다	to work
읽다	to read
잃어버리다	to lose
입구	entrance
입다	to wear, put on (clothes)
있다	1. to be (existence);
	2. to have
잊다	to forget
자다	to sleep
자동 응답기	answering machine
자동차	automobile
자라다	to grow up
자르다	to cut
자리	1. seat;
	2. digit
자연	nature
자전거	bicycle
자주	often, frequently
자취	living on one's own
자취하다	to live on one's own
자켓	jacket
작년	last year
작다	to be small (in size)
잔	glass, cup
잔치	feast, party
잘	well
잘라 드리다 *hum.*	to cut (something for someone)
잘라 주다 *plain*	to cut (something for someone)
잘생기다	to be handsome
잠	sleep
잠깐만	for a short time
잠실	Jamsil
잠을 자다	to sleep
잠이 들다	to fall asleep
잡다	to catch, grab

잡지	magazine
잡채	*japchae*
잡히다	to be caught
장(을) 보다	to buy one's groceries
장갑	gloves
장거리 전화	long-distance call
장롱	closet
장마	rainy season
장소	place, location
장학금	scholarship
장화	boots
재미없다	to be uninteresting
재미있다	to be interesting, fun
재즈	jazz
저	that (over there)
저 *hum.*	I (=나 *plain*)
저기	over there
저녁	1. evening;
	2. dinner
저어	uh (expression of hesitation)
저절로	automatically
저희 *hum.*	we/us/our (=우리 *plain*)
적극적이다	to be positive
적다	1. to be few, scarce;
	2. to write down
적어도	at least
적응	adaptation
적응하다	to adapt
전	before
전공	major
전공하다	to major
전기공학	electrical engineering
전부	all together
전세계	the whole world
전통	tradition
전통 문화	traditional culture
전통 찻집	traditional teahouse
전하다	to tell, convey
전화	telephone
전화번호	telephone number
전화비	telephone bill
전화하다	to make a telephone call
절	Buddhist temple
점심	lunch
점원	clerk, salesperson
점퍼	jumper/jacket
젓가락	chopsticks
정가	regular price
정도	approximate

정류장	(bus) stop	줄이다	to shorten
정리	arrangement	중간	the middle
정리하다	to arrange, organize	중고 가구	used furniture
정말	really	중고품	used merchandise
정원	yard, garden	중국	China
정육점	butcher shop	중부 지방	the central districts
정장	suit, formal dress	중식	Chinese food
정치학	political science	중심지	the pivot, center
정확하다	to be accurate	중앙 우체국	Central Post Office
제*hum.*	my (=내*plain*)	중에서	between, among
제과점	bakery	중요하다	to be important
제일	first, most	중학교	middle school
제주도	Jeju Island	중학생	middle school student
조그맣다	to be small	즐겁다	to be joyful
조금	a little (=좀)	즐기다	to enjoy
조심하다	to be careful	지갑	wallet
조용하다	to be quiet	지겹다	to be boring
졸다	to doze off	지금	now
졸리다	to be sleepy	지나가다	to pass by
졸업	graduation	지난	last, past
졸업하다	to graduate	지내다	to get along
졸업식	commencement	지다	1. to lose;
좀	a little (contraction of		2. to go down (the sun)
	조금)	지도	map
좁다	to be narrow	지방	region, district
종업원	employee	지역 번호	area code
종이	paper	지정하다	to appoint
좋다	to be good, nice	지키다	to guard, protect
좋아하다	to like	지하도	underpass
좌석	seat	지하 상가	underground market
죄송하다	to be sorry	지하철	subway
주	week	직원	staff, employee
주다	to give	직장인	office worker
주로	mostly, mainly	직접	directly
주말	weekend	질문	question
주무시다*hon.*	to sleep (=자다*plain*)	짐	luggage, load
주문하다	to order	집	home, house
주민등록번호	Resident Registration	집어넣다	to put something in
	number	짜다	to be salty
주민등록증	Resident Registration	짜리	worth
	card	짧다	to be short
주소	address	째	ordinal numbers
주스	juice	쪽	1. page;
주유소	gas station		2. side, direction
주인	owner	쭉	straight
주인공	main character	쯤	about, around
주차장	parking lot	찍다	to take (a photo)
죽다	to die	찜질방	Korean dry sauna
준비	preparation	차	1. car;
준비하다	to prepare		2. tea

Korean	English
차고	garage
차다	to be cold
차도	street, road
차비	fare (bus, taxi)
차차	gradually
착하다	to be good-natured, kindhearted
참	1. really, truly; 2. by the way
참기름	sesame oil
창가 좌석	window seat
찾다	1. to find, look for; 2. to withdraw(money)
책	book
책방	bookstore
책상	desk
책장	bookshelf, bookcase
처음	the first time
천천히	slow(ly)
첫	first
청바지	blue jeans
청소	cleaning
청소기	vacuum cleaner
청소하다	to clean
초등학교	elementary school
초등학생	elementary school student
초록색	green
최고	the highest
최저	the lowest
추워지다	to get colder
축구	soccer
축구하다	to play soccer
축하하다	to congratulate
출구	exit
출발	departure
출발하다	to depart
춤	dance
춤(을) 추다	to dance
춥다	to be cold
취미	hobby
층	floor, layer (counter)
치다	1. to play (tennis); 2. to play (piano, guitar)
치마	skirt
치약	toothpaste
친구	friend
친절하다	to be kind, considerate
친하다	to be close (to)
칠판	blackboard

Korean	English
침대	bed
침실	bedroom
칫솔	toothbrush
카드	card
카메라	camera
캐나다	Canada
캠퍼스	campus
커피	coffee
커피숍	coffee shop, café
컴퓨터	computer
컴퓨터 랩	computer lab
케이블카	cable car
케이크	cake
켜다	to play (violin)
켤레	pair (counter)
코미디	comedy
코트	coat
콘서트	concert
콘택트 렌즈	contact lens
콜라	cola
콩나물	bean sprout
쿠바	Cuba
크게	loud(ly)
크다	to be big
크리스마스	Christmas
큰술	tablespoon
큰아버지	uncle (father's older brother)
클래스	class
클래식	classical music
클럽	club
키	height
키가 작다	to be short
키가 크다	to be tall
타고 가다	to go riding
타고 다니다	to come/go riding
타고 오다	to come riding
타다	to get in/on, ride
타이레놀	Tylenol
태권도	Taekwondo
태어나다	to be born
택배	delivery service
택시	taxi
택시비	taxi fare
테니스	tennis
테니스장	tennis court
테이프	tape
텔레비전	television
토마토	tomato
토요일	Saturday

통화	phone call	하숙방	a room in a boardinghouse
통화하다	to make a phone call	하숙비	boarding expenses
트럭	truck	하숙집	boardinghouse
특별하다	to be special	하얗다	to be white
특히	particularly	하와이	Hawai'i
틀다	to turn on, switch on, play (music)	학교	school
티셔츠	T-shirt	학기	academic term
티켓	ticket	학년	school year
파	scallion	학비	tuition fees
파란색	blue	학생	student
파랗다	to be blue	학생회관	student center
파티	party	한	one (with counter)
팔다	to sell	한국	Korea
팔리다	to be sold	한국말	the Korean language
팬	pan	한국어	the Korean language
펜	pen	한국학	Korean studies
펴다	to open, unfold	한글	Korean alphabet
편도	one-way trip	한글날	Hangul Day
편리하다	to be convenient	한라산	Halla Mount
편안하다	to be comfortable	한복	Korean traditional dress
편의점	convenience store	한식	Korean food
편지	letter	한인타운	Koreatown
편하다	to be comfortable, convenient	한테	to (a person or an animal)
포근하다	to be warm	한테서	from (a person or an animal)
포장	packing		
폭포	waterfall	할머니	grandmother
표	ticket	할아버지	grandfather
표지판	sign	할인	discount
풀다	to relieve	함께	together, along with
풋볼	football	항공료	airfare
프랑스	France	항상	always
프로	program	핸드폰	cellular phone
피곤하다	to be tired	햄버거	hamburger
피다	to bloom	행	destined for
피시방	Internet café	행복하다	to be happy
피아노	piano	헤드폰	headphones
피우다	to smoke	헤어지다	to break up
피자	pizza	현관	(front) entrance
필요하다	to be necessary	현금	cash
하고	1. and (with nouns); 2. with	현재	the present
		형	the older brother of a male
하나	one		
하나도	(not) at all	형님 *hon.*	the older brother of a male
하늘	sky		
하늘색	sky blue	형제	sibling(s)
하다	to do	호박	pumpkin, squash
하루	(one) day	호선	subway line
하루 종일	all day	호주	Australia

호텔	hotel	환승하다	to transfer (a ride)
혹시	by any chance	회사	company
혼나다	to have a hard time	횡단보도	crosswalk
혼자	alone	후	after
홍콩	Hong Kong	후추	black pepper
화랑	gallery	휴게실	lounge
화려하다	to be fancy, colorful	휴일	holiday, day off
화면	screen	휴지	toilet paper
화씨	Fahrenheit	흐려지다	to get cloudy
화요일	Tuesday	흐리다	to be cloudy
화장실	bathroom, restroom	흰색	white
화장품	cosmetics	힘(이) 들다	to be hard
환승	transfer		

English-Korean Glossary

0 (zero)	영
0 (zero)	공 (phone #)
1	일
2	이
3	삼
4	사
about	에 대해서
about, around	쯤
academic term	학기
accessories	액세서리
accident	사고
according to	에 따라
account	계좌
action	액션
A.D.	서기
adapt [to]	적응하다
adaptation	적응
address	주소
adult, (one's) elders	어른
a few days	며칠
after	후
after a long time	오래간만
afternoon	오후
again	다시
age	나이 plain
	연세 hon.
air	공기
air-conditioner	에어컨
airfare	항공료
airplane	비행기
airport	공항
aisle	복도
Alaska	알래스카
alcoholic beverage	술
Alien Registration number	외국인등록 번호
a little	조금
	좀
a little later	이따가
all	다
	모두
all day	하루 종일
all together	전부
almost	거의
alone	혼자
already	벌써
also, too	도
alteration	수선
always	항상
a.m.	오전
a moment ago	방금
and	그리고
and (joins nouns)	와/과
	하고
and, also, too	또
animal (counter)	마리
answer	답
	대답
answer [to]	대답하다
answering machine	자동 응답기
antique	골동품
a pair of (counter)	벌
apartment	아파트
appetite	식성
apple	사과
appoint [to]	지정하다
approximate	정도
approximately	약
architecture	건축학
area code	지역 번호
arrange [to]	정리하다
arrive [to]	도착하다
art	예술
articles, goods	물품
Asia	아시아
Asian studies	동양학
ask [to]	묻다
ask a favor [to]	부탁하다
at, in, on (time)	에
at all [not]	하나도
at least	적어도
attend [to]	다니다
Australia	호주
automatically	저절로
automobile	자동차
autumn, fall	가을
a while ago	아까
back, behind	뒤
bag	가방
bakery	제과점
ballpoint pen	볼펜
bank	은행
barber shop	이발소
bargain sale	바겐 세일

baseball	야구	be cool, refreshing [to]	시원하다
baseball stadium	야구장	be correct [to]	맞다
basketball	농구	be crowded [to]	복잡하다
basketball game	농구 시합	bed	침대
bath	목욕	be dangerous [to]	위험하다
bathe [to]	목욕하다	be dark [to]	어둡다
bathroom, restroom	화장실	be delicious [to]	맛있다
battery	배터리	be deprived of [to]	뺏기다
B.C.	기원전	be different [to]	다르다
be (equation) [to]	이다	be difficult [to]	어렵다
be (existence) [to]	있다	be dirty [to]	더럽다
be (existence), stay [to]	계시다hon.	be diverse [to]	다양하다
be accurate [to]	정확하다	bedroom	침실
beach	바닷가	be dry [to]	건조하다
be all right, okay [to]	괜찮다	be easy [to]	쉽다
be amazing [to]	신기하다	beef	소고기
bean sprout	콩나물	be excited [to]	신나다
beauty salon	미용실	be excused [to]	실례하다
be bad [to]	나쁘다	be expensive [to]	비싸다
be beautiful [to]	아름답다	be familiar [to]	익숙하다
be big [to]	크다	be famous [to]	유명하다
be bitten [to]	물리다	be fancy, colorful [to]	화려하다
be bitter [to]	쓰다	be far [to]	멀다
be black [to]	까맣다	be fast [to]	빠르다
be bland [to]	싱겁다	be fat [to]	뚱뚱하다
be blocked [to]	막히다	be few, scarce [to]	적다
be blue [to]	파랗다	be foggy [to]	끼다
be bored [to]	심심하다	before	전
be boring [to]	지겹다	be formed [to]	생기다
be born [to]	태어나다	begin [to]	시작하다
be bright [to]	밝다	be glad [to]	반갑다
be busy [to]	바쁘다	be good, nice [to]	좋다
be careful [to]	조심하다	be good-natured [to]	착하다
be caught [to]	잡히다	be handsome [to]	잘생기다
because of	때문에	be happy [to]	행복하다
be changed [to]	바뀌다	be hard [to]	힘(이) 들다
be cheap [to]	싸다	be healthy [to]	건강하다
be clean [to]	깨끗하다	be heavy [to]	무겁다
be clear [to]	맑다	be high [to]	높다
be close (to) [to]	친하다	be hot [to]	덥다
be close, near [to]	가깝다		뜨겁다
be closed [to]	닫히다	be hot and humid [to]	무덥다
be cloudy [to]	흐리다	be how [to]	어떻다
be cold [to]	차다	be hungry [to]	배(가) 고프다
	춥다	be identical [to]	똑같다
become [to]	되다	be important [to]	중요하다
become cooler [to]	시원해지다	be in fashion [to]	유행하다
be comfortable [to]	편안하다	be insufficient [to]	부족하다
	편하다	be interesting, fun [to]	재미있다
be convenient [to]	편리하다	be joyful [to]	즐겁다

be joyful, glad [to]	기쁘다	be thick [to]	두껍다
be kind, considerate [to]	친절하다	be thin [to]	얇다
be late [to]	늦다	be thirsty [to]	목(이) 마르다
be light [to]	가볍다	be tired [to]	피곤하다
be lonely [to]	외롭다	be to one's liking [to]	마음에 들다
be long [to]	길다	between	사이
be low [to]	낮다	between, among	중에서
below the freezing point	영하	be ugly [to]	못생기다
be many, much [to]	많다	be uncomfortable [to]	불편하다
be narrow [to]	좁다	be undesirable [to]	싫다
be neat [to]	단정하다	be uninteresting [to]	재미없다
be necessary [to]	필요하다	be used [to]	쓰이다
be noisy [to]	시끄럽다	beverage	음료수
be open [to]	열리다	be warm [to]	따뜻하다
be over, finished [to]	끝나다		포근하다
be passive [to]	소극적이다	be well [to]	안녕하다
be positive [to]	적극적이다	be white [to]	하얗다
be pretty [to]	예쁘다	be wished [to]	기다려지다
be quiet [to]	조용하다	be yellow [to]	노랗다
be red [to]	빨갛다	be young [to]	어리다
be sad [to]	슬프다	bicycle	자전거
	아쉽다	biology	생물학
be safe [to]	안전하다	birthday	생일 *plain*
be salty [to]	짜다		생신*hon.*
be scary, scared [to]	무섭다	bite [to]	물다
be seen, visible [to]	보이다	black	검정색
be short [to]	짧다	black (=까망)	까만색
be short in height [to]	키가 작다	blackboard	칠판
be sick [to]	아프다	black pepper	후추
be similar [to]	비슷하다	bloom [to]	피다
be skinny [to]	마르다	blouse	블라우스
be sleepy [to]	졸리다	blow [to]	불다
be slim [to]	날씬하다	blue	파란색
be small (in size) [to]	작다	blue jeans	청바지
	조그맣다	boarding expenses	하숙비
be so [to]	그렇다	boardinghouse	하숙집
be sold [to]	팔리다	body	몸
be sorry [to]	미안하다	boil [to]	끓다
	죄송하다		끓이다
be sour [to]	시다	book	책
be spacious, wide [to]	넓다	bookshelf, bookcase	책장
be special [to]	특별하다	bookstore	책방
be spicy [to]	맵다		서점
be stylish, attractive [to]	멋있다	boots	장화
be surprised [to]	놀라다	borrow [to]	빌리다
be sweet [to]	달다	Boston	보스톤
be tall in height [to]	키가 크다	bottom [the], below	밑
be tasteless [to]	맛없다	bowling	볼링
be thankful [to]	감사하다	box	박스
	고맙다		상자

bread	빵	carrot	당근
break [to]	깨지다	carry around [to]	갖고 다니다
break down [to]	고장나다	case	경우
breakdown	고장	cash	현금
breakfast	아침	catch, grab [to]	잡다
break up [to]	헤어지다	cellular phone	핸드폰
bring [to]	갖고 오다	Celsius	섭씨
bring and put down	갖다 놓다	cent	센트
somewhere [to]		center [the], pivot	중심지
bring/take something	갖다 드리다	central districts [the]	중부 지방
to someone [to]		Central Post Office [the]	중앙 우체국
bring/take something	갖다 주다	century	세기
to someone [to]		chair	의자
broadcasting station	방송국	change (clothes) [to]	갈아 입다
Broadway theater	브로드웨이	change (money)	거스름돈
	극장	change (vehicles) [to]	갈아 타다
brush one's teeth [to]	이(를) 닦다	change, switch [to]	바꾸다
Buddhism	불교	check, bill	계산서
Buddhist temple	절	Chicago	시카고
building	건물	child	아이
	빌딩	China	중국
building, structure	건축물	Chinese food	중식
Bulguksa	불국사	choose, select [to]	고르다
bundle, bunch (counter)	단	chopsticks	젓가락
bus	버스	Christmas	크리스마스
but, however	그런데	church	교회
	그렇지만	cigarette	담배
butcher shop	정육점	city	도시
buy [to]	사다	city hall	시청
buy and eat [to]	사 먹다	city hall station	시청역
buy one's groceries [to]	장(을) 보다	class	반
by any chance	혹시		클래스
by chance, accident	우연히	classical music	클래식
by means of	으로	classroom	교실
by the way	그런데, 근데	clean [to]	청소하다
	참	cleaners	세탁소
cable car	케이블카	cleaning	청소
cake	케이크	clerk, salesperson	점원
calendar	달력	clock, watch	시계
call [to]	걸다	close [to]	닫다
camera	카메라	close, cover [to]	덮다
campus	캠퍼스	closet	장롱
Canada	캐나다	clothes	옷
cannot	못	clothing habits	의생활
cap, hat	모자	clothing store	옷가게
capital city	수도	cloud	구름
car	차	club	클럽
card	카드	coat	코트
care of health	몸조리	coffee	커피

coffee shop, café	커피숍	crossroads, intersection	사거리
cola	콜라	cry [to]	울다
collect [to]	모으다	Cuba	쿠바
college, university	대학	culture	문화
	대학교	cut [to]	자르다
college student	대학생	cut (something for	잘라 드리다
color	색, 색깔	someone) [to]	
come [to]	오다	cut (something	잘라 주다*plain*
comedy	코미디	for someone) [to]	
come/go riding [to]	타고 다니다	cut down [to]	깎다
come in [to]	들어오다	Dabo Tower	다보탑
come on foot [to]	걸어오다	daily life, living	생활
come out [to]	나오다	dance	춤
come out to greet	마중 나오다	dance [to]	춤(을) 추다
someone [to]		date	날짜
come riding [to]	타고 오다		데이트
comic book	만화책	date [to]	데이트하다
comic book rental store	만화방		사귀다
commencement	졸업식	date of birth	생년월일
company	회사	daughter	딸*plain*
computer	컴퓨터		따님*hon.*
computer lab	컴퓨터 랩	dawn	새벽
concert	음악회	day	날
	콘서트	day (counter)	일
condiment, seasoning	양념	day [one]	하루
congratulate [to]	축하하다	day after tomorrow [the]	모레
connect, link [to]	연결하다	daytime	낮
connection, link	연결	degree	도
construction	공사	deliver [to]	배달하다
contact	연락	delivery	배달
contact [to]	연락하다	delivery service	택배
contact lens	콘택트 렌즈	depart [to]	출발하다
contain [to]	들어있다	department store	백화점
continue [to]	계속되다	departure	출발
continuously	계속	desk	책상
convenience store	편의점	destined for	행
cook [to]	요리하다	develop, grow [to]	발달하다
cooked rice	밥	development	발달
cooking	요리	dialect	사투리
cosmetics	화장품	dictionary	사전
cost money [to]	돈이 들다	die [to]	죽다
cost of living	물가	digit	자리
country	나라	diligently	열심히
course, class	수업	dining table	식탁
course, subject	과목	dinner	저녁
cracker	과자	directly	바로
craftwork	공예품		직접
credit card	신용 카드	disappear [to]	없어지다
cross [to]	건너다	discount	할인

dish	그릇	education	교육학
dishwashing	설거지	egg	계란
dishwashing [to do]	설거지하다	electrical engineering	전기공학
dislike [to]	싫어하다	elementary school	초등학교
distance	거리	elementary school	초등학생
do [to]	하다	student	
doctor	의사	elevator	엘리베이터
dog	개	e-mail	이메일
do homework [to]	숙제하다	employee	종업원
dollar	달러	engagement	약속
	불	English language [the]	영어
domestic flight	국내선	enjoy [to]	즐기다
Dongdaemun Market	동대문시장	enter [to]	들어가다
do not	안	entrance	입구
door	문	entrance [front]	현관
dormitory	기숙사	envelope	봉투
do the laundry [to]	빨래하다	et cetera	등
downstairs	아래층	Europe	유럽
downtown	시내	evening	저녁
doze off [to]	졸다	event	일
drama	드라마	every day	날마다
draw [to]	그리다		매일
drawer	서랍	every month	매달
dream a dream [to]	꿈(을) 꾸다	every week	매주
dress [one-piece]	원피스	every year	매년
dress shirt	와이셔츠	exercise	연습 문제
dress shoes	구두		운동
drink [to]	마시다	exercise [to]	운동하다
drive [to]	운전하다	exit	출구
driver	기사	experience	경험
driver's license	운전 면허	eyeglasses	안경
driving	운전	eyes	눈
drugstore	약국	face	얼굴
drum	드럼	fact, truth	사실
during	동안	factory	공장
each	각	Fahrenheit	화씨
each other	서로	fall (down) [to]	넘어지다
early	일찍	fall asleep [to]	잠이 들다
earn (money) [to]	벌다	fall foliage	단풍
earn money [to]	돈을 벌다	family	가족
earring	귀걸이	fare (bus, taxi)	차비
east	동	farming	농사
East Coast	동부	fashion, trend	유행
East Hall	이스트 홀	fast, quickly	빨리
eat [to]	드시다*hon.*	father	아버지
	먹다*plain*	feast, party	잔치
eat out [to]	외식하다	fee, fare	요금
economics	경제학	feeling	기분
economy-class seat	일반석	fight [to]	싸우다

find, look for [to]	찾다	furniture store	가구점
find out, check out [to]	알아보다	gain age [to]	나이가 들다
fire station	소방서	gallery	화랑
first	첫	game	게임
first, beforehand	먼저	game, match	시합
first, most	제일	Gangwon region	강원
first birthday [the]	돌	garage	차고
first-class seat	일등석	garlic	마늘
first time [the]	처음	gas station	주유소
fish	생선	gather [to]	모이다
fishery	어업	generally, mostly	대체로
fit [to]	맞다	get, turn into [to]	되다
flesh, fat	살	get along [to]	지내다
floor	바닥	get around [to]	다니다
floor, layer (counter)	층	get busier [to]	바빠지다
floor heating system	온돌	get cloudy [to]	구름이 끼다
flower	꽃		흐려지다
flower shop	꽃집	get colder [to]	추워지다
fog	안개	get in/on, ride [to]	타다
food	음식	get lower [to]	낮아지다
food cost	음식값	get married [to]	결혼하다
food expenses	식비	get off [to]	내리다
foot	발	get up [to]	일어나다
football	풋볼	girlfriend	여자 친구
for, per	에	give [to]	드리다 *hum.*
for a long time	오랫동안		주다 *plain*
for a short time	잠깐만	give a present, gift [to]	선물하다
foreign country	외국	glass, cup	잔
foreign language	외국어	gloves	장갑
foreigner	외국인	go [to]	가다
for example	예를 들어	go and get back [to]	다녀 오다
forget [to]	잊다	go down (the sun) [to]	지다
four days	나흘	go down [to]	내려가다
France	프랑스	gold ring	금반지
free of charge	무료	golf	골프
freeze [to]	얼다	good fortune	복
freshman	1학년	go on foot [to]	걸어가다
Friday	금요일	go out [to]	나가다
friend	친구	go out to greet	마중 나가다
from (a person or an animal)	한테서	someone [to]	
		go riding [to]	타고 가다
from (location)	에서	go up [to]	올라가다
from (time)	에서	grade	성적
from (time) . . .	부터	gradually	차차
from next time	다음부터(는)	graduate [to]	졸업하다
front [the]	앞	graduate school	대학원
fruit	과일	graduate student	대학원생
function, work [to]	되다	graduation	졸업
furniture	가구	gram	그램

grandfather	할아버지
grandmother	할머니
green	초록색
green tea	녹차
greet [to]	인사하다
greeting	인사
grow up [to]	자라다
guard, protect [to]	지키다
guest, customer	손님
guitar	기타
Gwanak Mountain	관악산
Gyeongju	경주
hair	머리
half	반
half price	반값
Halla Mount	한라산
hamburger	햄버거
hand	손
Hangul Day	한글날
happen, break out	(noun)나다
hardship	고생
have [to]	있다
have, catch a cold [to]	감기에 걸리다
have a difficult time [to]	고생하다
have a full stomach [to]	배(가) 부르다
have a hard time [to]	혼나다
have a meal [to]	식사하다
Hawai'i	하와이
head	머리
headphones	헤드폰
heat [to]	달구다
heating	난방
heel	굽
height	키
hello (on the phone)	여보세요
help	도움
help [to]	돕다
	도와 주다 *plain*
	도와 드리다 *hum.*
here	여기
highest [the]	최고
high-rise building	고층빌딩
high school	고등학교
high school student	고등학생
highway, freeway	고속도로
hike [to]	등산하다
hiking	등산

history	역사
hobby	취미
holiday, day off	휴일
home, house	집 *plain*
	댁 *hon.*
hometown	고향
homework	숙제
honey, dear	여보
Hong Kong	홍콩
horror movie	공포 영화
hospital	병원
hotel	호텔
hot shredded-beef soup	육개장
hour, o'clock	시
how	어떻게
how long/much	얼마
how long/much	얼마나
how many, what (with a counter)	몇
hurry [to]	서두르다
hurt [to]	다치다
I	나 *plain*
	저 *hum.*
ice	얼음
ice cream	아이스크림
ice hockey	아이스하키
identification card	신분증
improve [to]	늘다
in, at (dynamic location)	에서
in, at, on (static location)	에
Incheon	인천
including	까지
inform [to]	알리다
in peace	안녕히
inquire [to]	물어보다
Insadong	인사동
inside [the]	안
instant noodles (ramen)	라면
international call	국제 전화
international flight	국제선
Internet	인터넷
Internet café	피시방
intersection, crossroads	네거리
interview	인터뷰
introduce [to]	소개하다
introduction	소개
I see	네
island	섬
Italy	이태리

item (counter)	개	lettuce	상추
jacket	자켓	library	도서관
Jamsil	잠실	lie down [to]	눕다
Japan	일본	like [to]	좋아하다
Japanese food	일식	linguistics	언어학
japchae	잡채	listen [to]	듣다
jazz	재즈	literature	문학
Jeju Island	제주도	live [to]	살다
journal	일기	live on one's own [to]	자취하다
juice	주스	living on one's own	자취
jumper/jacket	점퍼	living room	거실
junior	3학년	London	런던
just, just in time	마침	long-distance call	장거리 전화
just, without any special	그냥	long time	오래
reason		look around,	구경하다
kalbi (spareribs)	갈비	sightsee [to]	
karaoke room	노래방	Los Angeles (L.A.)	로스 앤젤레스
key	열쇠	lose [to]	잃어버리다
kimchi	김치	lose, be defeated [to]	지다
kimpab	김밥	loud(ly)	크게
kitchen	부엌	lounge	휴게실
know [to]	알다		라운지
Korea	한국	love	사랑
Korean Air	대한항공	love [to]	사랑하다
Korean alphabet	한글	lowest [the]	최저
Korean dry sauna	찜질방	luck, fortune	운
Korean food	한식	luggage, load	짐
Korean language	한국말	lunar calendar	음력
	한국어	lunch	점심
Korean studies	한국학	magazine	잡지
Koreatown	한인타운	mail (a letter, parcel) [to]	부치다
lab	랩	mail service	우편
lack [to]	모자라다	main character	주인공
lamp	램프	major	전공
last, past	지난	major [to]	전공하다
last night	어젯밤	make [to]	만들다
last year	작년	make a phone call [to]	통화하다
late	늦게		전화하다
later	나중에	make friends [to]	사귀다
laugh [to]	웃다	man	남자
law	법학	many, several	여러
learn [to]	배우다	map	지도
leave [to]	떠나다	market	마켓
leave (a message) [to]	남기다	marketplace	시장
left side	왼쪽	marriage	결혼
lend [to]	빌려주다	mart	마트
less	덜	master bedroom	안방
lesson, chapter	과	match, game	경기
letter	편지	match, suit [to]	어울리다

meal	밥	musical instrument	악기
	식사	musical performance	연주
mean, signify [to]	뜻하다	my	제hum.
meantime	그동안		내plain
meat	고기	naengmyŏn (cold	냉면
mechanical engineering	기계 공학	buckwheat noodles)	
medicine	약	Nam Mountain	남산
meet [to]	만나다	name	성함hon.
memorable	인상적		이름 plain
memorize [to]	외우다	national holidays	국경일
memory	기억	nature	자연
menu	메뉴	navy blue, indigo	남색
merchandise, stuff	물건	nearby, vicinity	근처
message	메시지	necklace	목걸이
meter	미터기	necktie	넥타이
Mexico	멕시코	neighborhood	동네
middle [the]	중간	new	새
middle, center [the]	가운데	New Year	새해
middle-aged woman	아주머니	New York	뉴욕
middle school	중학교	newly	새로
middle school student	중학생	news	뉴스
milk	우유	newspaper	신문
million	백만	newspaper publisher	신문사
mind, heart	마음	next, following	다음
minute (counter)	분	next year	내년
miss, long for [to]	그립다	night	밤
mister	아저씨	no	아니요
mom	엄마	noodles	면
Monday	월요일	north	북
money	돈	not be (existence) [to]	없다
month (counter)	개월	not be (negative	아니다
	월	equation) [to]	
	달	not have [to]	없다
moon	달	nothing but, only	밖에
more	더	not know [to]	모르다
more or less	다소	not N1 but N2	말고
morning	아침	not really	별로
most [the]	가장	not to be, not do [to]	않다
mostly, mainly	주로	novel	소설
motel	모텔	now	지금
mother	어머니	now	이젠(이제+는)
mountain climber	등산객	number	번호
move [to]	이사하다		숫자
move, shift [to]	옮기다	number (counter)	번
movie	영화	number of times	번
movie theater	극장	object particle	을/를
much, many	많이	of	의
muffler	목도리	office	사무실
museum	박물관	office worker	직장인
music	음악	often, frequently	자주

oh	아
	어
Oh! Oh my! Dear me!	어머
okay	네
old days [the]	옛날
older brother of a female [the]	오빠
older brother of a male [the]	형
older brother of a male [the]	형님 *hon.*
older sister of a female [the]	언니
older sister of a male [the]	누나
Olympics	올림픽
one	하나
one (with counter)	한
one portion	일 인 분
one-way trip	편도
onion	양파
only	만
open [to]	열다
open, unfold [to]	펴다
opera	오페라
oral exam	구두 시험
order [to]	주문하다
order (food) [to]	시키다
ordinal numbers (counter)	번째
	째
other side [the]	건너편
outside	밖
outside [the]	야외
oversleep	늦잠
over there	저기
owner	주인
pack [to]	싸다
pack, bag	봉지
packing	포장
page	쪽
pair	켤레
pan	팬
pants	바지
paper	종이
parcel, package	소포
parents	부모님
park	공원
parking lot	주차장
particularly	유난히
	특히

part-time job	아르바이트
party	파티
pass away [to]	돌아가시다 *h*
pass by [to]	지나가다
passport	여권
pay (money) [to]	돈을 내다
pear	배
pedestrian crossing	횡단보도
pen	펜
pencil	연필
people	분 *hon.*
people (counter)	명 *plain*
perform on a musical instrument [to]	연주하다
period	시대
person, people	사람
personality	성격
phone call	통화
photo, picture	사진
physics	물리학
piano	피아노
pibimbap	비빔밥
picture, painting	그림
pizza	피자
place, location	곳
	데
	장소
place, spot	군데
plan	계획
plan [to]	계획하다
play (piano, guitar) [to]	치다
play (tennis) [to]	치다
play (violin) [to]	켜다
play, drama	연극
play, not work [to]	놀다
play baseball [to]	야구하다
play basketball [to]	농구하다
playground	운동장
play soccer [to]	축구하다
plural particle	들
police	경찰
police station	경찰서
political science	정치학
popularity	인기
population	인구
postage	우편 요금
postal code	우편 번호
postbox	우체통
postcard	엽서

postman	우체부	registered (mail)	등기
post office	우체국	regular	보통
potato	감자	regular price	정가
practice	연습	relationship	사이
practice [to]	연습하다	relatively	비교적
preparation	준비	relieve [to]	풀다
prepare [to]	준비하다	remain [to]	남다
present [the]	현재		남아있다
present, gift	선물	remember [to]	기억하다
president	대통령	repeat after [to]	따라하다
presidential election	대통령 선거	reply	답장
price	가격	reply [to]	답장하다
	값	resemble [to]	닮다
probably, perhaps	아마	reservation	예약
problem	문제	reserve [to]	예약하다
professor	교수님	Resident Registration	주민등록증
professor's office	연구실	card	
program	프로	Resident Registration	주민등록번호
promise	약속	number	
psychology	심리학	rest [to]	쉬다
pub, bar	술집	restaurant	식당
public [the]	대중		음식점
pulgogi (roast meat)	불고기	return (something	돌려
pumpkin, squash	호박	to someone) [to]	드리다*hum.*
put forth effort [to]	수고하다	return (something	돌려
put in [to]	넣다	to someone) [to]	주다*plain*
put on [to]	얹다	return (to) [to]	돌아가다
put something down	놓아 주다	return, come back [to]	돌아오다
for someone [to]		review	복습
put something in [to]	집어넣다	ride pass, ticket	승차권
question	질문	right away, soon	곧
quick(ly)	어서	right side	오른쪽
radio	라디오	ring	반지
rain	비	rise, come up [to]	뜨다
rain [to]	비(가) 오다	rock music	록
rainy season	장마	rock-paper-scissors	가위바위보
read [to]	독서하다	room	방
	읽다	room in a	하숙방
reading	독서	boardinghouse	
really, truly	정말	roommate	룸메이트
	참	roughly	대충
receipt	영수증	rough map	약도
receive [to]	받다	round-trip	왕복
recipe	만드는 법	run [to]	뛰다
red	빨간색	Russia	러시아
red-pepper paste	고추장	sale	세일
refrigerator	냉장고	sandals	샌들
regards	안부	sandwich	샌드위치
region, district	지방	Saturday	토요일

sauna	사우나	side dishes	반찬
scallion	파	sidewalk	인도
scarf	목도리	sightseeing	구경
scenery, view	경치	sign	표지판
scholarship	장학금	sign, signature	사인
school	학교	Silla	신라
school uniform	교복	sincerely yours	올림
school vacation	방학	sing [to]	노래 부르다
school year	학년		노래하다
science	과학	sing (a song) [to]	부르다
screen	화면	singer	가수
sea	바다	single room	독방
search for [to]	구하다	sit [to]	앉다
season	계절	size	사이즈
season [to]	양념하다	ski	스키
seat	자리	ski [to]	스키 타다
	좌석	skirt	치마
second	두 번째	sky	하늘
see [to]	뵙다 *hum.*	sky blue	하늘색
see, look, watch [to]	보다 *plain*	sleep	잠
self-identification	본인 확인	sleep [to]	자다 *plain*
sell [to]	팔다		주무시다 *hon.*
send [to]	보내다		잠을 자다
senior	4학년	sleeve	소매
Seokga Tower	석가탑	slice [to]	썰다
Seokguram (stone cave)	석굴암	slipper	슬리퍼
Seorak Mount	설악산	slow(ly)	천천히
Seoul	서울	smoke [to]	피우다
Seoul Tower	서울타워	snow	눈
Seoul National	서울대	snow [to]	눈(이) 오다
University Station	입구역	so, therefore	그래서
service	서비스	soap	비누
sesame oil	참기름	soccer	축구
set	세트	Social Security number	사회보장
sex, gender	성별		번호
shape	모양	socks, stockings	양말
shirt	셔츠	sofa	소파
shoes	신발	soft tofu stew	순두부찌개
shop [to]	쇼핑하다	solar calendar	양력
shopping	쇼핑	some kind of	무슨
shopping district	상가	someone	누가
shorten [to]	줄이다		누구
shorts	반바지	something	뭐
show	쇼	sometime	언제
show, represent [to]	나타내다	sometimes	가끔
shower	샤워	somewhere	어디
sibling(s)	형제	son	아들
side, beside [the]	옆	song	노래
side, direction	쪽	soon	금방

sophomore	2학년	study room	공부방
sound, noise	소리	style	스타일
soup	스프	subject particle	께서 *hon.*
south	남		이/가 *plain*
South America	남미	subway	지하철
Southeast Asia	동남아	subway line	호선
Southern	남부	suddenly	갑자기
soybean-paste stew	된장찌개	sugar	설탕
soy sauce	간장	suit, formal dress	정장
spaghetti	스파게티	summer	여름
Spain	스페인	Sunday	일요일
speak [to]	말하다	supermarket	슈퍼(마켓)
speech, words	말씀 *hon.*	surely, certainly	꼭
	말 *plain*		반드시
spend time [to]	보내다	sushi	스시
spinach	시금치	sweater	스웨터
spoon	숟가락	swim [to]	수영하다
spoons and chopsticks	수저	swimming	수영
sports	스포츠	swimming pool	수영장
sports shoes, sneakers	운동화	Sydney	시드니
spread [to]	깔다	table	상
spring	봄	tablespoon	큰술
staff, employee	직원	Taekwondo	태권도
stairs	계단	take [to]	갖고 가다
stamp	우표	take (a photo) [to]	찍다
stand [to]	서다	take [time] [to]	걸리다
star	별	take, carry [to]	가져가다
station	역	take a course [to]	듣다
stick, affix [to]	붙이다	take a shower [to]	샤워하다
stir-fry [to]	볶다	take off, undress [to]	벗다
stomach, abdomen	배	talk, chat	이야기
stop [bus]	정류장		얘기
stop, pull over [to]	세우다	talk, chat [to]	이야기하다
stop by [to]	들르다		얘기하다
store	가게	tangerine	귤
	상점	tape	테이프
store signs	간판	taste [to]	맛보다
straight	쭉	taxi	택시
straight, upright	똑바로	taxi fare	택시비
street, road	거리	tea	차
	차도	teach [to]	가르치다
	길	teacher	선생님
stress	스트레스	teacher's wife	사모님
student	학생	telephone	전화
student abroad	유학생	telephone bill	전화비
student center	학생회관	telephone number	전화번호
studio apartment	원룸	television	텔레비전
study	공부	tell, convey [to]	전하다
study [to]	공부하다	temperature	기온

temple	사찰	toothpaste	치약
tennis	테니스	topic particle ('as for')	은/는
tennis court	테니스장	top side [the], above	위
test, exam	시험	toward, to	으로
textbook	교과서	town shuttle bus	마을 버스
than	보다	tradition	전통
that	그	traditional culture	전통 문화
that (over there)	저	traditional holidays	명절
then, if so	그럼	traditional Korean dress	한복
then, in that case	그러면	traditional teahouse	전통 찻집
there	거기	traffic	교통
these days	요새	traffic light	신호등
	요즘	traffic sign	교통 표지판
thief	도둑	train	기차
thing	것	transfer	환승
	거	transfer (a ride) [to]	환승하다
things to eat	먹거리	transportation card	교통카드
things to watch	볼거리	travel [to]	여행하다
thinly	얇게	travel, trip	여행
this	이	travel agency	여행사
	이거 (=이것)	truck	트럭
this time	이번	T-shirt	티셔츠
this way	이쪽(으로)	Tuesday	화요일
this year	올해	tuition fees	학비
thread	실	turn [to]	돌다
three days	사흘	turn in (homework) [to]	내다
thriller	스릴러	turn on, switch on,	틀다
Thursday	목요일	play (music) [to]	
ticket	티켓	two	둘
	표	two (with counter)	두
ticket office	매표소	two days	이틀
tie [to]	매다	Tylenol	타이레놀
time	때	uh (expression of	저어
time, hour (duration)	시간	hesitation)	
to (a person)	한테	umbrella	우산
	께 hon.	uncle (father's older	큰아버지
to (destination)	에	brother)	
to/until/through (time)	까지	underground market	지하 상가
today	오늘	underpass	지하도
tofu	두부	understand [to]	이해하다
together	같이	understand,	알아듣다
together, along with	함께	recognize [to]	
toilet paper	휴지	uniform	유니폼
Tokyo	도쿄	Union Building	유니온 빌딩
tomato	토마토	United Kingdom [the]	영국
tomorrow	내일	United States [the]	미국
too much	너무	up to (location)	까지
tooth	이	use [to]	사용하다
toothbrush	칫솔		쓰다

used furniture	중고 가구	what	뭐
used merchandise	중고품		무엇
usually	보통	what, what kind of	무슨
utilize [to]	이용하다	what date	며칠
vacuum cleaner	청소기	what matter	웬일
Vancouver	밴쿠버	what place, where	어디
vegetable	야채	when	언제
vending machine	발매기	which	어느
very, really	아주	which, what kind of	어떤
very much	굉장히	white	흰색
	무척	who	누구
violin	바이올린	who	누가 (누구+가)
visa	비자	whole world [the]	전세계
vocabulary	단어	why	왜
voice	목소리	win [to]	이기다
volume (counter)	권	wind	바람
wait [to]	기다리다	window seat	창가 좌석
walk [to]	걷다	winter	겨울
walk around [to]	걸어다니다	wish, want [to]	원하다
wallet	지갑	with	하고
want to [to]	고 싶다	withdraw (money) [to]	찾다
wardrobe, closet	옷장	without doing anything	그만
wash dishes [to]	설거지하다	further	
washing machine	세탁기	woman	여자
wash one's face [to]	세수하다	won (Korean currency)	원 (₩)
wash one's hands [to]	손(을) 씻다	work	일
water	물	work [to]	일하다
waterfall	폭포	World Cup	월드컵
way	길	worry [to]	걱정하다
wealthy person	부자	worry, concern	걱정
wear, put on	입다	worth	짜리
(clothes) [to]		worth, value	어치
wear (footwear) [to]	신다	Wow!	와
wear (glasses, gloves,	끼다	wrap [to]	싸다
rings) [to]		write [to]	쓰다
wear headgear [to]	쓰다	write down [to]	적다
weather	날씨	yard	마당
weather forecast	일기예보		정원
wedding	결혼식	yeah	응*plain*
Wednesday	수요일	year (counter)	년
week	주	years old	살
weekend	주말	yellow	노란색
weight	무게	yes, I see, okay	네/예
well	잘	yesterday	어제
Well; It's hard to say	글쎄요	yet, still	아직
west	서		아직도
Western-style (food)	양식	you	너*plain*
we/us/our	우리*plain*	younger brother	남동생
	저희*hum.*		

younger sibling	동생	Youngseo region	영서
younger sister	여동생	zoo	동물원
youngest child	막내		